Decoding the TOEFL® iBT

Basic

WRITING

INTRODUCTION

For many learners of English, the TOEFL® iBT will be the most important standardized test they ever take. Unfortunately for a large number of these individuals, the material covered on the TOEFL® iBT remains a mystery to them, so they are unable to do well on the test. We hope that by using the *Decoding the TOEFL® iBT* series, individuals who take the TOEFL® iBT will be able to excel on the test and, in the process of using the book, may unravel the mysteries of the test and therefore make the material covered on the TOEFL® iBT more familiar to themselves.

The TOEFL® iBT covers the four main skills that a person must learn when studying any foreign language: reading, listening, speaking, and writing. The *Decoding the TOEFL® iBT* series contains books that cover all four of these skills. The *Decoding the TOEFL® iBT* series contains books with three separate levels for all four of the topics as well as the *Decoding the TOEFL® iBT Actual Test* books. These books are all designed to enable learners to utilize them to become better prepared to take the TOEFL® iBT. This book, *Decoding the TOEFL® iBT Writing Basic*, covers the writing aspect of the test. It is designed to help learners prepare for the Writing section of the TOEFL® iBT.

Decoding the TOEFL® iBT Writing Basic can be used by learners who are taking classes and also by individuals who are studying by themselves. It contains two parts, each of which contains ten chapters. Part A covers the Integrated Writing Task while Part B covers the Independent Writing Task. There is also one actual test at the end of the book. Each chapter has either two Integrated tasks or two Independent questions. It also contains exercises designed to help learners understand how to write the best possible essays for the Writing section. The passages and questions in *Decoding the TOEFL® iBT Writing Basic* are lower levels than those found on the TOEFL® iBT. Individuals who use *Decoding the TOEFL® iBT Writing Basic* will therefore be able to prepare themselves not only to take the TOEFL® iBT but also to perform well on the test.

We hope that everyone who uses *Decoding the TOEFL® iBT Writing Basic* will be able to become more familiar with the TOEFL® iBT and will additionally improve his or her score on the test. As the title of the book implies, we hope that learners can use it to crack the code on the TOEFL® iBT, to make the test itself less mysterious and confusing, and to get the highest grade possible. Finally, we hope that both learners and instructors can use this book to its full potential. We wish all of you the best of luck as you study English and prepare for the TOEFL® iBT, and we hope that *Decoding the TOEFL® iBT Writing Basic* can provide you with assistance during the course of your studies.

Michael A. Putlack
Stephen Poirier

TABLE
OF
CONTENTS

Part A **Integrated Writing Task**

Part B **Independent Writing Task**

ABOUT THE TOEFL® iBT WRITING SECTION

How the Section Is Organized

The writing section is the last part of the TOEFL® iBT and consists of two portions: the Integrated Writing Task and the Independent Writing Task. The Integrated Writing Task requires test takers to explain how a short reading passage and lecture are related while the Independent Writing Task requires test takers to explain their opinions about a given situation. Test takers have 20 minutes to complete the Integrated Writing Task. For the Independent Writing Task, they have 30 minutes.

The writing section tests the ability of test takers to organize information clearly. The responses do not have to be creative or original. They just need to be succinct and direct. The most important thing test takers can do to boost their score is to present their ideas clearly by using relevant examples. Strong support and vivid details are essential for earning a top score.

Changes in the Writing Section

There are no major changes in the Writing section. However, in the Independent Writing Task, the directions tend to be longer than before on average. The question also often asks not only about a general opinion but also about a specific situation. This can be seen as a measure to prevent test takers from writing memorized essays. At the end of the question, there are directions that prohibit the writing of a memorized example. Therefore, it is important that test takers practice writing essays based on their own ideas instead of trying to memorize model essays.

Question Types

TYPE 1 The Integrated Writing Task

The Integrated Writing Task consists of three parts. Test takers begin by reading a passage approximately 230 to 300 words in length for 3 minutes. Following this, test takers listen to a lecture that either supports or contradicts the reading. Finally, test takers are given 20 minutes to write their essays. The essays should be between 150 and 225 words in length. During this time, the reading passage will reappear on the computer screen. Again, it is important to remember that test takers are not expected to present any new ideas in their essays. Instead, test takers must summarize the lecture and explain its relationship with the reading passage by providing examples from both.

ABOUT THE
TOEFL® iBT
WRITING SECTION

There are five possible writing tasks test takers will be presented with, but they all require test takers to summarize the lecture and to explain how it either supports or contradicts the reading.

If the listening passage challenges or contradicts the reading passage, the tasks will be presented in one of the following ways:

- Summarize the points made in the lecture, being sure to explain how they cast doubt on specific points made in the reading passage.

  cf. This question type accounts for most of the questions that have been asked on the TOEFL® iBT so far.

- Summarize the points made in the lecture, being sure to explain how they challenge specific claims/arguments made in the reading passage.

- Summarize the points made in the lecture, being sure to specifically explain how they answer the problems raised in the reading passage.

If the listening passage supports or strengthens the reading passage, the tasks will be presented in one of the following ways:

- Summarize the points made in the lecture, being sure to specifically explain how they support the explanations in the reading passage.

- Summarize the points made in the lecture, being sure to specifically explain how they strengthen specific points made in the reading passage.

TYPE 2 The Independent Writing Task

The Independent Writing Task is the second half of the TOEFL® iBT writing section. Test takers have 30 minutes to write an essay explaining their options about a given question. Typically, an effective response is between 300 and 400 words in length. In order to earn a top score, test takers must clearly present their ideas by using logical arguments and effective supporting examples. Strong responses generally include an introductory paragraph with a clear thesis statement, two or three supporting paragraphs with focused topic sentences, and a brief concluding paragraph.

There are three possible writing tasks you will be presented with, but they all ask you to express your opinion about an important issue.

For the agree/disagree type, the task will be presented in the following way:

- Do you agree or disagree with the following statement?
  [A sentence or sentences that present an issue]
  Use specific reasons and examples to support your answer.
  cf. This question type accounts for most of the essay topics that have been asked on the TOEFL® iBT so far.

For the preference type, the task will be presented in the following way:

- Some people prefer X. Others prefer Y. Which do you prefer? Use specific reasons and examples to support your choice.

For the opinion type, the task will be presented in the following way:

- [A sentence or sentences that state a fact]
  In your opinion, what is one thing that should be . . . ? Use specific reasons and examples to support your answer.

HOW TO USE THIS BOOK

Decoding the TOEFL® iBT Writing Basic is designed to be used either as a textbook in a classroom environment or as a study guide for individual learners. There are 2 parts with 10 chapters each in this book. Each chapter provides 2 sample tasks or questions. There are 4 or 5 sections in each chapter, which enable you to build up your skills on a particular writing task. At the end of the book, there is one actual test of the Writing section of the TOEFL® iBT.

Part A Integrated Writing Task

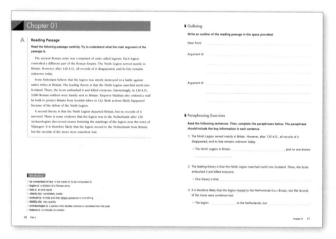

A | Reading Passage

This section contains a reading passage between 160 and 190 words long. There is a vocabulary section with definitions of difficult words or phrases in the passage. There are also sections for outlining and paraphrasing/summarizing to make sure you understand the material you read and can condense it.

B | Listening Lecture

This section contains a listening lecture between 160 and 190 words long. There is a section for note-taking so that you can write down the key information you hear in the lecture. There is also a paraphrasing/summarizing section to make sure you can condense the information that you heard.

C | Combining the Main Points

This section contains 2 excerpts each from the reading passage and listening lecture. You should read the excerpts and then use the information in them to complete each sentence. Then, complete the sample essay on the next page by using the outline you wrote and the notes you took.

D | Completing the Essay

This part has space to write an essay in response to the question. There are some expressions included to help you with your writing.

iBT Practice Test

This part contains a reading passage, a listening lecture, and a question. There is also space to write an essay in response to the question.

Part B | Independent Writing Task

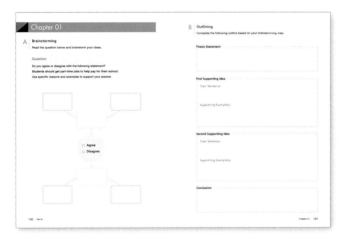

A | Brainstorming

This section contains a question and space for brainstorming to prepare to write your answer.

B | Outlining

This part has space for an outline that will describe what information will be included in the introduction, body, and conclusion of the essay.

C | Completing the Essay

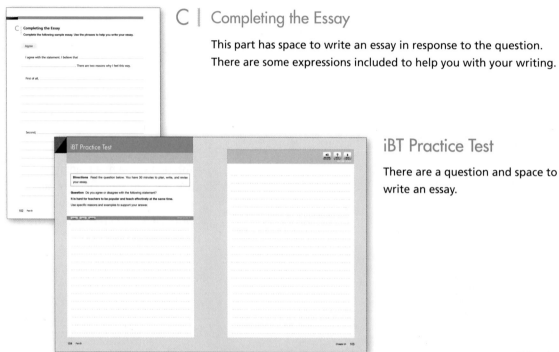

This part has space to write an essay in response to the question. There are some expressions included to help you with your writing.

iBT Practice Test

There are a question and space to write an essay.

● Actual Test (at the end of the book)

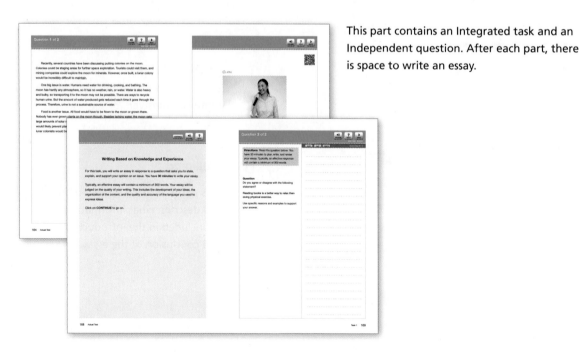

This part contains an Integrated task and an Independent question. After each part, there is space to write an essay.

Part **A**

Integrated Writing Task

Integrated Writing Task

About the Question

The Integrated Writing Task contains three parts. The first part is a reading passage that is around 230 to 300 words long. You are given 3 minutes to read the passage. Next, you will hear a lecture that either supports the reading passage or goes against it in some manner. Last, you will be given 20 minutes to write an essay on the reading passage and listening lecture. Your essay should be 150 to 225 words long. While you are writing your essay, you will be able to see the reading passage on the screen. To write your essay, simply provide a summary of the lecture and explain how it is connected to the reading passage. You should be sure to use the examples that are provided in the two passages. However, avoid using any new ideas or examples that do not appear in either of the passages. Your essay must be taken solely from the information presented in the two passages.

There are five possible writing tasks that may be presented to you. All of them require that you summarize the lecture and explain how it supports or goes against the reading passage. The vast majority of passages have the lecture contradicting, casting doubt on, or challenging the issues that are mentioned in the reading passage. Very few lectures support the reading passage.

If the listening passage challenges or contradicts the reading passage, the tasks will be presented in one of the following ways:

- Summarize the points made in the lecture, being sure to explain how they cast doubt on specific points made in the reading.

    cf. This question type accounts for most of the questions that have been asked on the TOEFL® iBT so far.

- Summarize the points made in the lecture, being sure to explain how they challenge specific claims/arguments made in the reading.

- Summarize the points made in the lecture, being sure to specifically explain how they answer the problems raised in the reading passage.

If the listening passage supports or strengthens the reading passage, the tasks will be presented in one of the following ways:

- Summarize the points made in the lecture, being sure to specifically explain how they support the explanations in the reading passage.

- Summarize the points made in the lecture, being sure to specifically explain how they strengthen specific points made in the reading passage.

The largest shark ever to live was the megalodon. It was more than sixteen meters long and had teeth seventeen centimeters long. It was a fearsome predator that went extinct around 1.6 million years ago. However, some people claim it still exists.

Many people claim there is video evidence proving there are megalodons. Some videos show enormous animals whose profiles resemble sharks swimming in the ocean. But these fish are much larger than any other known sharks. In one video, a great white shark is swimming. Suddenly, a shark with a similar body style but which is much larger than the great white shark swims by. This is most likely a megalodon.

Scientists estimate that humans have only explored around five percent of the world's oceans. There are places such as the Mariana Trench that are several thousand meters deep. Most of them have never been explored or visited by humans. It is probable that there are megalodons swimming in these areas. They are still alive, but they avoid places humans go. So they are not seen by anyone.

🎧 A00

| Script | **M Professor:** Someone asked me my opinion on the megalodon and whether or not it's still alive. My answer is no. It went extinct more than a million years ago and no longer swims in the oceans.

Now, uh, there are plenty of videos online showing what people claim are megalodons. Well, many of them are fakes. Watch some of those videos, and you'll notice how blurry the sharks frequently are. In other cases, the animals people are calling megalodons are other species of sharks. For example, I've seen videos of basking sharks, but people call them megalodons. Simply put, there are no videos showing megalodons today.

Some people claim that megalodons live deep beneath the surface. Well, those people know nothing about the megalodon. The fossil evidence shows that it lived in shallow water near coasts. It was a huge fish, so it needed to consume large amounts of food each day. The coast is where its food supply was. Its nursing grounds were also near shore. If there were megalodons swimming near beaches, I'm sure we would have seen them by now.

Directions You have 20 minutes to plan and write your response. Your response will be judged on the basis of the quality of your writing and on how well your response presents the points in the lecture and their relationship to the passage. Typically, an effective response will be 150-225 words.

Question Summarize the points made in the lecture, being sure to explain how they cast doubt on specific points made in the reading passage.

Sample Essay

The lecture and the reading passage discuss whether the megalodon is extinct. The megalodon was a huge shark more than sixteen meters long. The author of the reading passage believes it is still alive. But the professor casts doubt on the arguments made in the reading passage.

First, the professor talks about videos that supposedly show megalodons. While the author of the reading passage claims they are real, the professor disagrees. He says many videos are fakes. They are often blurry, so it is hard to see the sharks. Other videos show basking sharks and other types of sharks, but people say they are megalodons.

After that, the professor discusses where the megalodon lives. In the reading passage, the author remarks that megalodons may live thousands of meters beneath the surface of the ocean. The professor says that is impossible. He points out that megalodon lived in shallow water near shore. It hunted and had its nursing grounds there. If megalodon was still alive, people would have seen it by now.

Chapter 01

A | Reading Passage

Read the following passage carefully. Try to understand what the main argument of the passage is.

The ancient Roman army was comprised of units called legions. Each legion controlled a different part of the Roman Empire. The Ninth Legion served mainly in Britain. However, after 120 A.D., all records of it disappeared, and its fate remains unknown today.

Some historians believe that the legion was utterly destroyed in a battle against native tribes in Britain. The leading theory is that the Ninth Legion marched north into Scotland. There, the Scots ambushed it and killed everyone. Interestingly, in 120 A.D., 3,000 Roman soldiers were hastily sent to Britain. Emperor Hadrian also ordered a wall be built to protect Britain from Scottish tribes in 122. Both actions likely happened because of the defeat of the Ninth Legion.

A second theory is that the Ninth Legion departed Britain, but no records of it survived. There is some evidence that the legion was in the Netherlands after 120. Archaeologists discovered stones featuring the markings of the legion near the town of Nijmegen. It is therefore likely that the legion moved to the Netherlands from Britain, but the records of the move were somehow lost.

Vocabulary

- [ ] **be comprised of** [phr] to be made of; to be composed of
- [ ] **legion** [n] a division of a Roman army
- [ ] **fate** [n] an end result
- [ ] **utterly** [adv] completely; totally
- [ ] **ambush** [v] to hide and then to attack someone or something
- [ ] **hastily** [adv] very quickly
- [ ] **archaeologist** [n] a person who studies cultures or societies from the past
- [ ] **feature** [v] to include; to contain

▌ Outlining

Write an outline of the reading passage in the space provided.

Main Point _____

Argument ❶ _____

_____

_____

Argument ❷ _____

_____

_____

▌ Paraphrasing Exercises

Read the following sentences. Then, complete the paraphrases below. The paraphrase should include the key information in each sentence.

1 The Ninth Legion served mainly in Britain. However, after 120 A.D., all records of it disappeared, and its fate remains unknown today.

→ The Ninth Legion in Britain _____, and no one knows

_____ .

2 The leading theory is that the Ninth Legion marched north into Scotland. There, the Scots ambushed it and killed everyone.

→ One theory is that _____ .

3 It is therefore likely that the legion moved to the Netherlands from Britain, but the records of the move were somehow lost.

→ The legion _____ to the Netherlands, but _____ .

B | Listening Lecture 🎧 A01

Listen to a lecture on the topic you just read about. Be sure to take notes while you listen.

■ Note-Taking

Main Point   _____

Argument ❶   _____

_____

_____

Argument ❷   _____

_____

_____

■ Paraphrasing Exercises

Read the following sentences. Then, complete the paraphrases below. The paraphrase should include the key information in each sentence.

1   Nobody knows what happened to the Roman Ninth Legion that was stationed in Britain.

    → _____ is a mystery.

2   If they had all been killed in one place, we would have found evidence of a mass grave.

    → If everyone was killed, _____.

3   An entire legion would have left much more archaeological evidence, like relics, than has been found in that region.

    → A legion would have left _____.

C Combining the Main Points

Read the following sentences from the reading passage and listening lecture. Then, combine each pair of sentences by using the given patterns.

1 **Reading** The leading theory is that the Ninth Legion marched north into Scotland. There, the Scots ambushed it and killed everyone.

Listening The most popular theory is that a Scottish army totally destroyed the legion in 120 A.D. But, well, there's no evidence of such a battle taking place. For instance, no mass graves have been found.

→ **According to the reading passage,** _____

_____ **. But the professor points out**

_____ **.**

2 **Reading** There is some evidence that the legion was in the Netherlands after 120. Archaeologists discovered stones featuring the markings of the legion near the town of Nijmegen.

Listening Second, while there's some evidence the Ninth Legion was in the Netherlands later, I believe this was a small unit of men, not the entire legion. An entire legion would have left much more archaeological evidence, like relics, than has been found in that region.

→ **The reading passage mentions** _____

_____ **. The professor, however, thinks** _____

_____ **. He remarks that** _____

_____ **.**

D | Completing the Essay

Complete the following sample essay which summarizes the points made in the lecture. Be sure to explain how they cast doubt on specific points made in the reading passage. Use the phrases to help you write your essay.

Both the lecture and the reading passage are about _____

_____. The professor's lecture _____ the arguments

made in the reading passage.

First, the professor doubts that _____

_____. According to the reading passage, _____

_____. But

the professor points out _____. He says that thousands of

men and horses would have died in one place. But he mentions that _____

_____. So the battle never happened.

Next, the professor does not believe _____.

The reading passage mentions _____

_____. The professor, however, thinks _____

_____. He remarks that little archaeological evidence is there.

He believes _____.

In the dry deserts of Peru are hundreds of strange drawings in the earth. These are the Nazca Lines, which are named after the people who created them. The drawings are huge and include lines, geometrical figures, and animals. Despite studying them for years, nobody knows exactly why the Nazca people made the lines.

Some scholars believe there is a connection with astronomy. They theorize that the Nazca people utilized the lines to study the stars to let them know the seasons for farming purposes. As a result, they were able to know when to plow the land, to plant the seeds, and to harvest their crops. The lines therefore served as something like a calendar for the Nazca people.

Other individuals subscribe to the theory that the Nazca Lines were used to honor the leaders of the Nazca people. The people drew the lines in the ground to show their respect for their rulers. According to them, it is likely that each animal or shape corresponded with a particular individual. Thus the lines were created over the course of hundreds of years as rulers came and went.

A02

Directions You have 20 minutes to plan and write your response. Your response will be judged on the basis of the quality of your writing and on how well your response presents the points in the lecture and their relationship to the passage. Typically, an effective response will be 150-225 words.

Question Summarize the points made in the lecture, being sure to explain how they challenge specific arguments made in the reading passage.

COPY   CUT   PASTE   Word Count : 0

A Reading Passage

Read the following passage carefully. Try to understand what the main argument of the passage is.

Yellowstone National Park in the United States sits on top of an enormous supervolcano. It last erupted around 640,000 years ago. There has been an increase in geological activity around the supervolcano in recent years. As a result, geologists believe the chances of the Yellowstone supervolcano erupting in the near future are high.

Geologists measure the rising and falling of the land around volcanoes. If the land is rising, it means that molten rock, called magma, underground is increasing in mass and pressure. Basically, the magma is pushing the land above it up. At Yellowstone, the land typically rises 1.5 centimeters a year. However, in some places, it has been rising as much as twenty centimeters a year. This indicates that an eruption will happen sooner rather than later.

The Yellowstone area has seen numerous earthquakes in recent years. Usually, it gets more than 1,000 minor earthquakes annually. But in one period in February 2018, there were hundreds of earthquakes in fewer than two weeks. None was major or caused any damage. However, the rapid increase in geological activity is a warning of an eruption that will come soon.

Vocabulary

- ☐ **supervolcano** *n* a volcano that explodes much more violently than a regular volcano
- ☐ **erupt** *v* to explode
- ☐ **geological** *adj* relating to the earth or ground
- ☐ **molten** *adj* melted
- ☐ **mass** *n* size
- ☐ **earthquake** *n* the sudden, and often violent, moving of the ground
- ☐ **annually** *adv* once a year; yearly
- ☐ **warning** *n* a notice that something bad may happen

◼ Outlining

Write an outline of the reading passage in the space provided.

Main Point   _____

Argument ❶   _____

  _____

  _____

Argument ❷   _____

  _____

  _____

◼ Paraphrasing Exercises

Read the following sentences. Then, complete the paraphrases below. The paraphrase should include the key information in each sentence.

1 Geologists believe the chances of the Yellowstone supervolcano erupting in the near future are high.

→ The Yellowstone supervolcano will _____ .

2 If the land is rising, it means that molten rock, called magma, underground is increasing in mass and pressure.

→ Rising land means _____ .

3 But in one period in February 2018, there were hundreds of earthquakes in fewer than two weeks. None was major or caused any damage.

→ _____ in fewer than two weeks in

February 2018.

B | Listening Lecture 🎧 A03

Listen to a lecture on the topic you just read about. Be sure to take notes while you listen.

■ Note-Taking

Main Point _____

Argument ❶ _____

_____

_____

Argument ❷ _____

_____

_____

■ Paraphrasing Exercises

Read the following sentences. Then, complete the paraphrases below. The paraphrase should include the key information in each sentence.

1 Some geologists believe that if it erupts, it could cause a global disaster that will kill hundreds of millions of people.

   → An eruption could _____ .

2 No magma has emerged from the ground, so we don't need to be worried yet.

   → There are no problems since _____ .

3 Swarms are common at Yellowstone, happening every few years. A large one took place in 1985, yet there was no eruption.

   → Swarms at Yellowstone _____

   are common.

C | Combining the Main Points

Read the following sentences from the reading passage and listening lecture. Then, combine each pair of sentences by using the given patterns.

1 **Reading** If the land is rising, it means that molten rock, called magma, underground is increasing in mass and pressure. Basically, the magma is pushing the land above it up. At Yellowstone, the land typically rises 1.5 centimeters a year. However, in some places, it has been rising as much as twenty centimeters a year.

Listening But note that this has happened at Yellowstone on numerous occasions. For instance, the most recent increase in the level of the land started ten years ago. And nothing has happened yet. No magma has emerged from the ground, so we don't need to be worried yet.

→ **According to the reading passage,** _____

_____ . **Some places at Yellowstone are rising rapidly, which**

indicates _____ . **But the professor points out that** _____

_____ . **He says** _____

_____ .

2 **Reading** But in one period in February 2018, there were hundreds of earthquakes in fewer than two weeks. None was major or caused any damage. However, the rapid increase in geological activity is a warning of an eruption that will come soon.

Listening Swarms are common at Yellowstone, um, happening every few years. A large one took place in 1985, yet there was no eruption.

→ **There was a swarm in 1985 that** _____ . **This goes against**

the argument in the reading passage. It claims that when there are _____

_____ , **an earthquake will happen soon.**

D | Completing the Essay

Complete the following sample essay which summarizes the points made in the lecture. Be sure to explain how they cast doubt on specific points made in the reading passage. Use the phrases to help you write your essay.

Both the lecture and the reading passage are about _____.

The author of the reading passage believes that _____. However, the

professor _____ the arguments in the reading passage in his lecture.

For starters, the professor talks about _____.

According to the reading passage, _____

_____. Some places at Yellowstone are rising rapidly, which

indicates _____. But the professor points out that _____

_____. He says _____.

Next, the professor talks about _____. He mentions that _____

_____. There was a swarm in 1985 that _____

_____. This _____ the argument in the reading

passage. It claims that when there are _____

_____, an earthquake will happen soon.

In the late 1400s, a large number of animals on New Zealand's South Island suddenly died. This happened when a powerful tsunami flooded large parts of the island. Experts today believe that a comet impact in the Pacific Ocean caused the tsunami.

The primary evidence for this theory is the Mahuika crater. This impact crater on the ocean floor south of New Zealand was discovered in 2003. Scientists determined its age by examining material known as tektites, which were around it. Tektites are glass beads that form when a comet hits an area. The tektites had little sediment on them, suggesting they were relatively new. Scientists have estimated that they are around 500 years old. That is about when the tsunami occurred.

Another indication that a comet hit the planet then comes from some Maori legends. The Maori are the native inhabitants of New Zealand. According to their stories, there was a huge fire in the sky one night. It supposedly happened around 500 years ago. The Maori legends about the fire describe how a comet would appear if it entered the Earth's atmosphere and hit the ground.

🎧 A04

Directions You have 20 minutes to plan and write your response. Your response will be judged on the basis of the quality of your writing and on how well your response presents the points in the lecture and their relationship to the passage. Typically, an effective response will be 150-225 words.

Question Summarize the points made in the lecture, being sure to explain how they cast doubt on specific points made in the reading passage.

COPY CUT PASTE   Word Count : 0

A Reading Passage

Read the following passage carefully. Try to understand what the main argument of the passage is.

Sharks are some of the most fearsome predators on the planet. In recent years, the number of attacks on humans has risen worldwide. It appears that they are deliberately seeking humans for food, so this is making sharks more dangerous to humans.

Every year, more and more shark attacks are being reported in the media. For instance, in recent times, shark attacks in Brazil, Australia, and Florida have received a great deal of media attention. In 2005, there were only sixty-one recorded attacks worldwide, and four were fatal. But the number of attacks started rising. In 2015, there were ninety-eight attacks while there were eighty-one attacks in 2016.

Recently, sharks have been sighted swimming closer to shore than ever before. They have also been seen in places they do not usually go. This may indicate that they are actively searching for humans. Even shallow water and river mouths are not safe for swimming in some places. At Port St. John's, South Africa, there were ten shark attacks from 2009 to 2015. Eight were deadly. Most of the attacks occurred in shallow water close to shore.

Vocabulary

- **fearsome** _adj_ frightening, often in a dangerous manner
- **predator** _n_ an animal that hunts other animals, often to eat them
- **deliberately** _adv_ on purpose
- **media** _n_ a collection of groups that report the news in newspapers or on TV, radio, and the Internet
- **worldwide** _adv_ around the world
- **fatal** _adj_ deadly
- **shallow** _adj_ being low in level; not deep
- **river mouth** _n_ the area where a river empties into an ocean or a sea

■ Outlining

Write an outline of the reading passage in the space provided.

Main Point   _____

Argument ❶   _____

            _____

            _____

Argument ❷   _____

            _____

            _____

■ Paraphrasing Exercises

Read the following sentences. Then, complete the paraphrases below. The paraphrase should include the key information in each sentence.

1   It appears that they are deliberately seeking humans for food, so this is making sharks more dangerous to humans.

     → Sharks are _____ humans, which makes them _____.

2   For instance, in recent times, shark attacks in Brazil, Australia, and Florida have received a great deal of media attention.

     → _____ shark attacks in _____ places have gotten _____.

3   Recently, sharks have been sighted swimming closer to shore than ever before. They have also been seen in places they do not usually go.

     → Sharks are swimming _____ and going to places _____

     _____.

B | Listening Lecture 🎧 A05

Listen to a lecture on the topic you just read about. Be sure to take notes while you listen.

▌ Note-Taking

Main Point _____

Argument ❶ _____

_____

_____

Argument ❷ _____

_____

_____

▌ Paraphrasing Exercises

Read the following sentences. Then, complete the paraphrases below. The paraphrase should include the key information in each sentence.

1 You know, some people believe shark attacks are rising because sharks are intentionally targeting humans. I don't agree though.

→ I do not agree that _____.

2 In the past, shark attacks were usually unreported unless they were fatal. Nowadays, every attack—fatal or not—is reported.

→ _____ were reported in the past, but _____

_____.

3 Many swimmers are going farther away from the beach, which is right where the sharks are.

→ Swimmers are going _____.

C | Combining the Main Points

Read the following sentences from the reading passage and listening lecture. Then, combine each pair of sentences by using the given patterns.

1 **Reading** In 2005, there were only sixty-one recorded attacks worldwide, and four were fatal. But the number of attacks started rising. In 2015, there were ninety-eight attacks while there were eighty-one attacks in 2016.

Listening In the past, shark attacks were usually unreported unless they were fatal. Nowadays, every attack—fatal or not—is reported. So it's possible there were more shark attacks in the past than today. We just don't know.

→ **The author of the reading passage claims that** _____.

From 2005 to 2015, the number of attacks _____. **The professor,**

however, says that in the past, _____.

He thinks it is possible that _____.

2 **Reading** Recently, sharks have been sighted swimming closer to shore than ever before. They have also been seen in places they do not usually go. This may indicate that they are actively searching for humans.

Listening Unfortunately, many swimmers are going farther away from the beach, which is right where the sharks are. They splash around in the water, making sharks think they're fish. So the sharks attack the swimmers. Most shark attacks are due to mistaken identity, not purposeful attacks.

→ **The professor points out that** _____

_____. **They are going to places where** _____. **The**

swimmers splash around, so the sharks _____.

These remarks _____ **the claim in the reading passage. It argues that** _____

_____ **in the hope of** _____.

D | Completing the Essay

Complete the following sample essay which summarizes the points made in the lecture. Be sure to explain how they challenge specific claims made in the reading passage. Use the phrases to help you write your essay.

The professor's lecture is on _____. While the author of the reading passage

believes that _____, the professor disagrees.

The professor first considers _____. The author of the reading

passage claims that _____. From 2005 to 2015,

_____. The professor, however,

says that in the past, _____. He thinks it is

possible that _____.

Next, the professor mentions _____. He points out

that _____. They are going to

places _____. The swimmers _____,

so the sharks _____. These remarks

challenge the claim in the reading passage. It argues that _____

_____.

The sperm whale has an organ in the top half of its head called the spermaceti organ. It produces a fluid called spermaceti. The exact purpose of both the organ and the fluid is presently a matter of debate.

One possibility is that spermaceti is used to help the sperm whale float on the water and to dive deep beneath it. Basically, the whale can heat or cool the spermaceti organ by drawing in cool water or by expelling it. By raising or lowering the temperature of this huge organ and its fluid, the whale changes the density of the fluid. This gives the whale more or less buoyancy. This, in turn, lets the whale more easily dive or rise.

A second possibility is that the spermaceti organ and the fluid are used for echolocation. Whales use echolocation to navigate and to find food. The sperm whale sends out a series of noises, which bounce off objects, return, and hit the whale's head. Perhaps the organ and fluid play a role in analyzing these echoes. By knowing where food or an obstacle is, the whale can eat or navigate better.

A06

Directions You have 20 minutes to plan and write your response. Your response will be judged on the basis of the quality of your writing and on how well your response presents the points in the lecture and their relationship to the passage. Typically, an effective response will be 150-225 words.

Question Summarize the points made in the lecture, being sure to explain how they cast doubt on specific points made in the reading passage.

COPY   CUT   PASTE

Word Count : 0

A | Reading Passage

Read the following passage carefully. Try to understand what the main argument of the passage is.

There are numerous ways to produce electricity on a large scale. Of these methods, the most ideal one is nuclear power. Nuclear power plants are capable of creating alternative energy which is both cheap and clean.

When nuclear power plants open in an area, the local residents always see their electricity bills decline rapidly. This happens mainly because of the fuel that nuclear power plants utilize to create electricity. Most of them run on plutonium and uranium. These two elements can produce energy for a long time, which helps lower the price of electricity.

A second advantage of nuclear power plants is that they are extremely clean. There is very little atmospheric venting from nuclear power plants. So they release few pollutants into the atmosphere. This is quite different from other power plants, such as those utilizing coal. They produce a tremendous amount of pollution and are bad for the environment. Modern nuclear power plants also do not release any harmful radiation because they are so safe. By not harming the environment with radiation, they are clean sources of energy.

Vocabulary

- ☐ **nuclear** *adj* relating to atomic energy or weapons
- ☐ **alternative energy** *n* energy that is not created by using fossil fuels such as gas, oil, or coal
- ☐ **decline** *v* to go down
- ☐ **advantage** *n* a benefit
- ☐ **atmospheric** *adj* relating to the air
- ☐ **venting** *n* the act of releasing something
- ☐ **pollutant** *n* something that can make an area dirty or polluted
- ☐ **radiation** *n* particles that are released by various radioactive elements

◼ Outlining

Write an outline of the reading passage in the space provided.

Main Point _____

Argument ❶ _____

_____

_____

_____

Argument ❷ _____

_____

_____

_____

◼ Paraphrasing Exercises

Read the following sentences. Then, complete the paraphrases below. The paraphrase should include the key information in each sentence.

1 Nuclear power plants are capable of creating alternative energy which is both cheap and clean.

→ Nuclear power plants can _____.

2 Most of them run on plutonium and uranium. These two elements can produce energy for a long time, which helps lower the price of electricity.

→ Plutonium and uranium can _____.

3 Modern nuclear power plants also do not release any harmful radiation because they are so safe.

→ Nuclear power plants _____ so are safe.

Listen to a lecture on the topic you just read about. Be sure to take notes while you listen.

■ Note-Taking

Main Point _____

Argument ❶ _____

_____

_____

Argument ❷ _____

_____

_____

■ Paraphrasing Exercises

Read the following sentences. Then, complete the paraphrases below. The paraphrase should include the key information in each sentence.

1 These days, lots of people are proposing that we create more energy by building nuclear power plants.

→ Many people want to _____ .

2 It costs billions of dollars to construct a single plant. That's an enormous expense which most places cannot afford.

→ It takes billions of dollars to build one plant, which is _____ .

3 Nuclear power is simply too dangerous. A single accident could harm millions of people and destroy the local environment.

→ Nuclear power is dangerous since _____ .

C   Combining the Main Points

Read the following sentences from the reading passage and listening lecture. Then, combine each pair of sentences by using the given patterns.

1   **Reading**   When nuclear power plants open in an area, the local residents always see their electricity bills decline rapidly. This happens mainly because of the fuel that nuclear power plants utilize to create electricity.

Listening   First, nuclear power is extremely expensive. Oh, sure, the local residents might get small electricity bills. But have you seen how expensive it is to build a nuclear power plant? It costs billions of dollars to construct a single plant. That's an enormous expense which most places cannot afford.

→ **According to the reading passage,** _____ .

As a result, people's electricity bills _____ **thanks to** _____ .

The professor agrees that _____ **. But she points out that**

_____ .

2   **Reading**   Modern nuclear power plants also do not release any harmful radiation because they are so safe. By not harming the environment with radiation, they are clean sources of energy.

Listening   But what about when there are accidents at nuclear power plants? Consider the meltdown of the reactor at Chernobyl in the Soviet Union. And how about the Fukushima reactor in Japan? The power plants at each place caused, um, a tremendous amount of damage to a widespread area.

→ **While the reading passage claims that** _____

_____ **, the professor disagrees. She brings up** _____ **such as those at**

_____ **. She mentions** _____ .

D | Completing the Essay

Complete the following sample essay which summarizes the points made in the lecture. Be sure to explain how they challenge specific arguments made in the reading passage. Use the phrases to help you write your essay.

The professor lectures against _____ for a couple of reasons.

In doing so, she _____ the two arguments made in the reading passage.

The first point she mentions is _____. According to the reading

passage, _____. As a result, _____

_____ thanks to nuclear power plants. The professor agrees that

_____. But she points out that _____

_____. She believes this is too expensive.

Second, the professor argues that _____

_____. While the reading passage claims that _____

_____, the professor disagrees. She brings up _____

_____. She mentions _____

_____. In her opinion, an accident at a nuclear power plant could _____

_____.

The current methods used to recycle bottles made of PET polymers, a type of plastic, are inefficient. However, a new enzyme was recently discovered. It can quickly degrade PET plastic to its original form and should help reduce pollution caused by plastic containers.

The enzyme is naturally occurring, and scientists have enhanced it to make it work even faster. When left alone, PET plastic takes hundreds of years to break down. But the new enzyme requires just a few days to do that. Right now, around one-third of all PET products cannot be recycled economically. The new enzyme, however, can break down all of these items. This will make recycling profitable.

In addition, the present recycling method for PET plastic merely produces a less viable plastic. After this plastic gets reused and recycled several times, it degrades so badly that it cannot be recycled anymore. However, plastic recycled after being exposed to the new enzyme will not have this problem. It will not degrade to the point that it eventually cannot be recycled. This will benefit the environment since less plastic will be thrown away.

🎧 A08

Directions You have 20 minutes to plan and write your response. Your response will be judged on the basis of the quality of your writing and on how well your response presents the points in the lecture and their relationship to the passage. Typically, an effective response will be 150-225 words.

Question Summarize the points made in the lecture, being sure to explain how they challenge specific claims made in the reading passage.

COPY CUT PASTE

Word Count : 0

A | Reading Passage

Read the following passage carefully. Try to understand what the main argument of the passage is.

Thanks to advances in technology, consumers no longer have to visit stores to do their shopping. Now, they can visit various websites and make purchases online. There are several advantages to online shopping.

One of the biggest advantages of online shopping is the convenience. People no longer need to visit stores far from their homes and then walk around them in search of items. Instead, they can look at a wide variety of products from the comfort of their homes or offices. To do online shopping, only a computer and a credit card are needed. Delivery is fast and cheap. And companies often deliver around the world, which widens the number of available products.

Online shopping is also good for job creation. First, manufacturers sell more products, so they hire more people to make items. This increases employment. Second, online vendors and packing and shipping facilities often employ large numbers of workers. For example, online retailer Amazon.com is building a new distribution center due to high volume. It will employ numerous people. Online shopping thus stimulates economic activity, creating a stronger economy.

Vocabulary

- ☐ **consumer** *n* a person who purchases goods or services
- ☐ **convenience** *n* ease; simplicity
- ☐ **delivery** *n* the act of taking something from one place to another
- ☐ **widen** *v* to increase in size or amount
- ☐ **manufacturer** *n* a maker of various products
- ☐ **retailer** *n* a seller of goods, usually in small amounts
- ☐ **distribution** *n* the act of transporting products to various places
- ☐ **stimulate** *v* to cause to increase

◪ Outlining

Write an outline of the reading passage in the space provided.

Main Point _____

Argument ❶ _____

_____

_____

Argument ❷ _____

_____

_____

◪ Paraphrasing Exercises

Read the following sentences. Then, complete the paraphrases below. The paraphrase should include the key information in each sentence.

1 Thanks to advances in technology, consumers no longer have to visit stores to do their shopping.

→ Technological advances mean _____.

2 People no longer need to visit stores far from their homes and then walk around them in search of items.

→ People do not need to _____.

3 First, manufacturers sell more products, so they hire more people to make items. This increases employment.

→ Manufacturers sell more _____ so hire more _____, increasing _____.

B | Listening Lecture 🎧 A09

Listen to a lecture on the topic you just read about. Be sure to take notes while you listen.

◼ Note-Taking

Main Point _____

Argument ❶ _____

_____

_____

Argument ❷ _____

_____

_____

◼ Paraphrasing Exercises

Read the following sentences. Then, complete the paraphrases below. The paraphrase should include the key information in each sentence.

1 And I understand the appeal of online shopping. However, if you ask me, retail shopping is the better choice.

→ I understand _____ but think _____ .

2 Another convenience of retail shopping is that stores are frequently located close to one another.

→ Retail stores are often _____ .

3 Many small towns also rely on retail stores and shopping malls for jobs for their residents.

→ Small towns need stores and malls to _____ .

C | Combining the Main Points

Read the following sentences from the reading passage and listening lecture. Then, combine each pair of sentences by using the given patterns.

1 **Reading** One of the biggest advantages of online shopping is the convenience. People no longer need to visit stores far from their homes and then walk around them in search of items. Instead, they can look at a wide variety of products from the comfort of their homes or offices.

Listening Another convenience of retail shopping is that stores are frequently located close to one another. Think about the local shopping mall as an example. There are more than 250 stores in a single building. People can find just about anything they need by visiting the mall.

→ **The professor points out that** _____ **, so people can**

_____ **. Her opinions** _____ **those in the**

reading passage. It argues that online shopping is convenient because _____

_____ **.**

2 **Reading** First, manufacturers sell more products, so they hire more people to make items. This increases employment. Second, online vendors and packing and shipping facilities often employ large numbers of workers.

Listening Consider how many people are employed at the mall downtown. When customers shop at the stores there, they are helping those establishments stay in business. Many small towns also rely on retail stores and shopping malls for jobs for their residents. Without customers shopping at them, those stores would close.

→ **The reading passage declares that** _____ **.**

The reason is that _____ **and that** _____

_____ **. But the professor mentions that** _____

_____ **. If people do not shop at them,** _____ **.**

D | Completing the Essay

Complete the following sample essay which summarizes the points made in the lecture. Be sure to explain how they challenge specific claims made in the reading passage. Use the phrases to help you write your essay.

The lecture and the reading passage are about _____. In the professor's opinion,

_____ is better than _____. Her views _____ the

claims made in the reading passage.

The professor begins by talking about _____. She

mentions that _____ before

buying them. The professor also points out that _____,

so people can _____. Her opinions _____

in the reading passage. It argues that online shopping is convenient because _____

_____.

The professor then discusses _____.

The reading passage declares that _____.

The reason is that _____ and that _____

_____. But the professor mentions that _____

_____. If people do not shop at them, _____

_____.

In 1929, the American stock market crashed, causing the Great Depression of the 1930s. According to economists, the Great Depression lasted so long because of the reaction of American consumers to the crisis. This is called the demand driven theory.

This theory states that there was less demand for products by consumers, so the depression became worse. Basically, people reacted to the stock market crash by saving their money. They were concerned about being unemployed in the future. This took a great deal of money out of circulation as people made fewer purchases. As demand for products went down, factories began making fewer products. This led to numerous bankruptcies and high unemployment.

Banks also failed since people were hoarding money. There were runs on banks as depositors withdrew their savings. This left banks with no cash to loan to individuals who wanted to start new businesses or make investments. With fewer people investing, the economy stalled. There were no businesses opening and no innovations being made. This worsened the situation and made the depression last more than a decade.

A10

Directions You have 20 minutes to plan and write your response. Your response will be judged on the basis of the quality of your writing and on how well your response presents the points in the lecture and their relationship to the passage. Typically, an effective response will be 150-225 words.

Question Summarize the points made in the lecture, being sure to explain how they challenge specific claims made in the reading passage.

COPY　　CUT　　PASTE

Word Count : 0

A | Reading Passage

Read the following passage carefully. Try to understand what the main argument of the passage is.

Most historians agree that the Vikings from Northern Europe were the first outsiders to reach the Americas. Christopher Columbus is also considered the runner up in this race. However, new evidence shows that the Chinese reached the Americas in the early fifteenth century. They accomplished this feat several decades before Columbus crossed the Atlantic Ocean.

During the early fifteenth century, China was an aggressive trading nation seeking new markets. It had many large oceangoing sailing ships. Large fleets of these ships sailed across the Indian Ocean to places in Arabia and Africa. It is highly likely that the Chinese also sent ships east across the Pacific Ocean. They could have easily reached North America.

There is even proof that the Chinese made it to North America thanks to a Chinese map that was made in 1418. It shows the entire world, including the Americas. It contains numerous details of the Americas that nobody in Europe knew about at that time. This map could only have been made by Chinese sailors who had visited the Americas.

Vocabulary

- ☐ **runner up** n a second-place finisher
- ☐ **evidence** n proof
- ☐ **feat** n an act; an accomplishment
- ☐ **decade** n a period lasting ten years
- ☐ **aggressive** adj competitive; making a great effort to excel at something
- ☐ **oceangoing** adj able to sail on the ocean out of sight of land
- ☐ **fleet** n a group of ships sailing together
- ☐ **detail** n a fact or information about someone or something

◢ Outlining

Write an outline of the reading passage in the space provided.

Main Point _____

Argument ❶ _____

_____

_____

Argument ❷ _____

_____

_____

◢ Paraphrasing Exercises

Read the following sentences. Then, complete the paraphrases below. The paraphrase should include the key information in each sentence.

1 However, new evidence shows that the Chinese reached the Americas in the early fifteenth century.

→ The Chinese _____ in the early _____.

2 It is highly likely that the Chinese also sent ships east across the Pacific Ocean. They could have easily reached North America.

→ The Chinese _____ sent ships across the Pacific Ocean that _____

_____.

3 There is even proof that the Chinese made it to North America thanks to a Chinese map that was made in 1418.

→ A Chinese map _____ proves _____.

B | Listening Lecture 🎧 A11

Listen to a lecture on the topic you just read about. Be sure to take notes while you listen.

◼ Note-Taking

Main Point _____

Argument ❶ _____

_____

_____

Argument ❷ _____

_____

_____

◼ Paraphrasing Exercises

Read the following sentences. Then, complete the paraphrases below. The paraphrase should include the key information in each sentence.

1 In recent years, some historians have been claiming that a fleet of Chinese ships sailed across the Pacific Ocean and made it to the Americas in the 1400s.

→ Some historians believe _____ .

2 The problem is that there's no evidence the Chinese landed in the Americas. No Chinese relics have been unearthed in the Americas.

→ No Chinese relics are in the Americas, so there is _____ .

3 And the map is based on a round Earth. But the Chinese didn't believe the Earth was round at that time.

→ The map shows a round Earth, but the Chinese _____ .

C Combining the Main Points

Read the following sentences from the reading passage and listening lecture. Then, combine each pair of sentences by using the given patterns.

1 Reading Large fleets of these ships sailed across the Indian Ocean to places in Arabia and Africa. It is highly likely that the Chinese also sent ships east across the Pacific Ocean. They could have easily reached North America.

Listening The problem is that there's no evidence the Chinese landed in the Americas. No Chinese relics have been unearthed in the Americas. Nor are there any historical records of Chinese ships visiting the Americas.

→ The reading passage argues that since the Chinese _____

_____ , they probably sent ships _____ , too.

The professor, however, notes that there are _____ in the Americas

or _____ proving ships sailed there.

2 Reading There is even proof that the Chinese made it to North America thanks to a Chinese map that was made in 1418. It shows the entire world, including the Americas.

Listening And the map is based on a round Earth. But, well, the Chinese didn't believe the Earth was round at that time. In all likelihood, that map is a fake made centuries later.

→ According to the reading passage, this map was made in China in _____ . It shows

_____ , including _____ . The professor calls the map a

_____ though. He says it shows a _____ , but the Chinese didn't believe

_____ then.

D | Completing the Essay

Complete the following sample essay which summarizes the points made in the lecture. Be sure to explain how they cast doubt on specific points made in the reading passage. Use the phrases to help you write your essay.

The professor lectures on whether _____

_____. The professor does not believe _____. He therefore _____

the claims made in the reading passage.

The professor's first point is that _____

_____. The reading passage argues that since the Chinese sent ships

west into the Indian Ocean, _____, too.

The professor, however, notes that _____

_____.

The professor's second point concerns _____. According to the reading passage, this

map was made in China in 1418. It shows _____, including _____.

The professor _____ though. He says it shows a round Earth, but the

Chinese _____. In addition, the Chinese

never _____, so he says they _____.

VOLUME   HELP   NEXT

HIDE TIME 00:03:00

In 1971, the Grolier Club, a New York book club, displayed a book written in the Mayan language. It is now called the Grolier Codex. Only three other Mayan books have ever been discovered. Each one was found in the nineteenth century. Due to the codex's unusual nature, many people consider it a fake.

The Grolier Codex was discovered in the 1960s. Is supposedly shows the movements of the planet Venus and dates from the thirteenth century. However, the Mayan glyphs in the book are not arranged like those in the other three books. Additionally, the Grolier Codex only has writing on one side of each page. The others have writing on both sides. These facts suggest that someone with a limited knowledge of the Mayan style forged the book.

The paper is made of tree bark, which the Mayans made books from. Yet the pages appear to have been cut recently. This indicates that the book is not as old as believed. Plus, many examples of blank Mayan bark paper have been discovered. In all likelihood, a forger utilized real Mayan paper to create a fake book.

A12

Directions You have 20 minutes to plan and write your response. Your response will be judged on the basis of the quality of your writing and on how well your response presents the points in the lecture and their relationship to the passage. Typically, an effective response will be 150-225 words.

Question Summarize the points made in the lecture, being sure to explain how they challenge specific claims made in the reading passage.

COPY   CUT   PASTE   Word Count : 0

A | Reading Passage

Read the following passage carefully. Try to understand what the main argument of the passage is.

In recent years, elephant conservation efforts in Africa have been highly successful. Many herds have increased in size. Unfortunately, these elephants are now encroaching on populated areas and endangering humans. These herds need to have their populations controlled. The best way to do that is to use birth control methods on them.

Scientists have devised a way to interrupt the birth cycle of female elephants. By injecting females with medicine, scientists can slow their birth rate. This will reduce the wild elephant population. This method will be somewhat slow to show results. However, in a few years, it will bring the elephant population under control.

Public opinion also needs to be considered. Some people have suggested culling herds by killing elephants. That would cause global outrage though. Using contraception is a more humane method of dealing with the issue. There is also public support for using contraception. In addition, nobody knows for certain how many elephants currently live in the wild. If too many elephants get culled, it could trigger an unstoppable population decline. Contraception, on the other hand, would allow for a more balanced control of the population.

Vocabulary

- □ **conservation** *n* the act of saving or preserving something
- □ **herd** *n* a large group of animals
- □ **encroach** *v* to move into an area owned or occupied by someone or something else
- □ **endanger** *v* to be a threat to someone or something
- □ **devise** *v* to think of; to invent
- □ **inject** *v* to insert a liquid into a body by using a needle
- □ **cull** *v* to kill, often in great numbers
- □ **humane** *adj* kindhearted; caring; compassionate

◢ Outlining

Write an outline of the reading passage in the space provided.

Main Point _____

Argument ❶ _____

_____

_____

Argument ❷ _____

_____

_____

◢ Paraphrasing Exercises

Read the following sentences. Then, complete the paraphrases below. The paraphrase should include the key information in each sentence.

1 These herds need to have their populations controlled. The best way to do that is to use birth control methods on them.

→ Birth control is the best _____ .

2 This method will be somewhat slow to show results. However, in a few years, it will bring the elephant population under control.

→ The method will be slow but will _____ .

3 Using contraception is a more humane method of dealing with the issue. There is also public support for using contraception.

→ Using contraception is _____ and has _____ .

B | Listening Lecture 🎧 A13

Listen to a lecture on the topic you just read about. Be sure to take notes while you listen.

▮ Note-Taking

Main Point   _____

Argument ❶   _____

_____

_____

Argument ❷   _____

_____

_____

▮ Paraphrasing Exercises

Read the following sentences. Then, complete the paraphrases below. The paraphrase should include the key information in each sentence.

1   These days, expanding elephant herds near population centers in Africa are causing problems. Some of these herds need to be culled.

→ Elephant herds are _____, so they _____.

2   They would be shot, so entire herds could be culled swiftly. This would allow a region to become elephant free in a short period of time.

→ Herds can be culled swiftly, so _____.

3   It would be a quick, humane way of dealing with the problem. The elephants wouldn't suffer and would be killed instantly.

→ It would be a _____ way to _____.

C | Combining the Main Points

Read the following sentences from the reading passage and listening lecture. Then, combine each pair of sentences by using the given patterns.

1 **Reading** By injecting females with medicine, scientists can slow their birth rate. This will reduce the wild elephant population. This method will be somewhat slow to show results. However, in a few years, it will bring the elephant population under control.

Listening By culling, I mean that some elephants should be killed. They would be shot, so entire herds could be culled swiftly. This would allow a region to become elephant free in a short period of time.

→ **According to the reading passage, contraception would** _____

_____. **But the professor believes** _____

_____. **She proposes** _____.

2 **Reading** Using contraception is a more humane method of dealing with the issue. There is also public support for using contraception. In addition, nobody knows for certain how many elephants currently live in the wild. If too many elephants get culled, it could trigger an unstoppable population decline. Contraception, on the other hand, would allow for a more balanced control of the population.

Listening So lots of people think culling is wrong. It would be a quick, humane way of dealing with the problem. The elephants wouldn't suffer and would be killed instantly. Culling is also cheaper and safer than using contraception.

→ **Next, the professor claims that culling the elephants is** _____. **This is in**

contrast to the reading passage. It states that using contraception is _____

and that it would _____.

D | Completing the Essay

Complete the following sample essay which summarizes the points made in the lecture. Be sure to explain how they challenge specific arguments made in the reading passage. Use the phrases to help you write your essay.

In her lecture, the professor talks about _____

_____. She challenges _____

when she speaks.

In the professor's opinion, _____. This differs from the

reading passage, which suggests _____. According to the reading passage,

contraception would slowly _____. But the

professor believes results are needed now. She _____

_____. That will enable people to _____,

and it will keep humans safe.

Next, the professor claims that _____.

This is _____ the reading passage. It states that _____

_____ and that _____. However,

the professor says that elephants _____ if they are shot. She also points out that

_____ would be dangerous. She thinks that male

elephants might _____.

The lionfish is a venomous invasive species that dwells in the Caribbean Sea and the Atlantic Ocean. Living in coral reefs, it has few predators. As a result, its population has grown out of control. It has become an ecological danger because it eats numerous other fish in coral reefs.

One way to control the lionfish population is to add it to people's diets. While the fish is venomous, it is edible if prepared properly. Only the fish's spines are venomous, and removing them is simple. Cooked lionfish tastes delicious and has less harmful mercury than other fish and plenty of healthy omega-3 fatty acids. Many restaurants in the Caribbean and the United States currently sell it. If eating lionfish becomes more widespread, its population can be controlled better.

There is an additional benefit to using the lionfish as a food fish. It will lessen the strain on other fish species, some of which are endangered. Humans are overfishing many regions. The common species they catch, including grouper and snapper, are declining in numbers. Replacing these fish with lionfish will let the populations of other fish grow.

A14

Directions You have 20 minutes to plan and write your response. Your response will be judged on the basis of the quality of your writing and on how well your response presents the points in the lecture and their relationship to the passage. Typically, an effective response will be 150-225 words.

Question Summarize the points made in the lecture, being sure to explain how they challenge specific claims made in the reading passage.

COPY   CUT   PASTE   Word Count : 0

A | Reading Passage

Read the following passage carefully. Try to understand what the main argument of the passage is.

The water hyacinth is a flowering plant currently causing problems in Louisiana, USA. The hyacinth grows in thick groups on the surface of water. This blocks sunlight, which kills other plants. It also reduces oxygen levels, so fish cannot breathe and then die.

Louisiana is dealing with this problem in three ways. One is by using pesticides. They are relatively cheap and effective. One study showed that pesticides have reduced the growth of the flower by approximately thirty percent in some waterways.

Another solution is to cut the plants and to remove them by hand. Many local communities in Louisiana do this and have found it effective at killing the plant. People volunteer to do this on their days off, so the cost is minimal. All they require is tools and time.

A third solution is the introduction of species that can harm the water hyacinth. Two insects—a type of weevil and an aquatic grasshopper, are known to eat or damage the plant. Weevils have been used there since the 1970s and have been fairly successful. The grasshopper is currently being studied to determine how effective it will be.

Vocabulary

- **block** *v* to prevent one thing from reaching another
- **oxygen** *n* the element that animals need to breathe to survive
- **pesticide** *n* a weed killer; poison that is used to kill certain plants
- **approximately** *adv* around; about
- **waterway** *n* a river, canal, or other body of water that ships travel on
- **volunteer** *v* to spend one's free time doing some kind of work for no money
- **minimal** *adj* small; minor
- **aquatic** *adj* relating to the water

Outlining

Write an outline of the reading passage in the space provided.

Main Point _____

Argument ❶ _____

_____

Argument ❷ _____

_____

Argument ❸ _____

_____

Paraphrasing Exercises

Read the following sentences. Then, complete the paraphrases below. The paraphrase should include the key information in each sentence.

1 One study showed that pesticides have reduced the growth of the flower by approximately thirty percent in some waterways.

→ Pesticides reduce the flower by _____.

2 Another solution is to cut the plants and to remove them by hand. Many local communities in Louisiana do this and have found it effective at killing the plant.

→ People often kill the plant by _____.

3 Two insects—a type of weevil and an aquatic grasshopper, are known to eat or damage the plant.

→ Some insects _____.

B | Listening Lecture 🎧 A15

Listen to a lecture on the topic you just read about. Be sure to take notes while you listen.

◾ Note-Taking

Main Point
_____

Argument ❶
_____

_____

Argument ❷
_____

_____

Argument ❸
_____

_____

◾ Paraphrasing Exercises

Read the following sentences. Then, complete the paraphrases below. The paraphrase should include the key information in each sentence.

1 First, pesticides have been used. They've done a good job, but they've also caused considerable amounts of harm to the environment.

    → Pesticides are _____ but _____.

2 When the plant is pulled out, small pieces tend to break off. These parts can survive and then grow into larger plants.

    → Some plant parts break off, _____, and then _____.

3 They don't harm the environment, but the hyacinth grows rapidly, so the insects can't eat enough to counter the new growth.

    → The insects cannot _____ since the hyacinth _____.

C | Combining the Main Points

Read the following sentences from the reading passage and listening lecture. Then, combine each pair of sentences by using the given patterns.

1 **Reading** One is by using pesticides. They are relatively cheap and effective. One study showed that pesticides have reduced the growth of the flower by approximately thirty percent in some waterways.

Listening First, pesticides have been used. They've done a good job, but they've also caused considerable amounts of harm to the environment. You see, the chemicals in the pesticides get into the water system and harm both plants and animals.

→ **The professor starts by talking about** _____.

According to the reading passage, they _____. **The**

professor agrees, but she states that _____,

so they harm plants and animals.

2 **Reading** Another solution is to cut the plants and to remove them by hand. Many local communities in Louisiana do this and have found it effective at killing the plant. People volunteer to do this on their days off, so the cost is minimal.

Listening When the plant is pulled out, small pieces tend to break off. These parts can survive and then grow into larger plants. As a result, cleared ponds and rivers often see renewed hyacinth growth in a short period of time.

→ **The reading passage claims that this is a** _____ **way to** _____

the plant. But the professor says that _____ **and**

quickly _____.

D | Completing the Essay

Complete the following sample essay which summarizes the points made in the lecture. Be sure to explain how they challenge specific claims made in the reading passage. Use the phrases to help you write your essay.

In her lecture, the professor discusses _____. She

mentions three ways that people _____. Her arguments _____

_____ made in the reading passage.

The professor starts by talking about _____.

According to the reading passage, _____. The professor

agrees, but she states that pesticides also damage the environment, so _____

_____.

Next, the professor brings up _____. The reading

passage claims that _____.

But the professor says that _____

_____.

Last, the professor lectures about _____

_____. She agrees with the reading passage that _____

_____. But she mentions that _____, so they are

mostly _____.

The blue iguana is an endangered lizard species living in the Cayman Islands in the Caribbean Sea. In recent years, it has suffered a major decline in its population for several reasons.

The Cayman Islands have a limited amount of space. Growing human populations took over the blue iguana's territory. The construction of roads, hotels, and houses pushed it out of its preferred habitats. By the 1980s, the blue iguana was limited to a small area on one island. With less living space, its food supply shrank, so its numbers grew smaller.

Another problem is the green iguana. Its numbers are far greater than those of the blue iguana. Each reptile eats vegetation, but green iguanas often damage gardens and trees. As the two species look similar, people frequently kill any iguanas, both blue and green, they see on their land. These actions have led to the deaths of numerous blue iguanas.

A third problem is that people captured and sold blue iguanas to tourists and zoos. The iguanas were then taken off the Caymans. Unfortunately, many people didn't take good care of them, so the iguanas often died.

🎧 A16

Directions You have 20 minutes to plan and write your response. Your response will be judged on the basis of the quality of your writing and on how well your response presents the points in the lecture and their relationship to the passage. Typically, an effective response will be 150-225 words.

Question Summarize the points made in the lecture, being sure to explain how they challenge specific claims made in the reading passage.

COPY   CUT   PASTE   Word Count : 0

A | Reading Passage

Read the following passage carefully. Try to understand what the main argument of the passage is.

Honeysuckle is a family of vines and shrubs native to North America and Eurasia. Botanists have identified around 180 species of honeysuckle. It grows in the wild, but it is also a popular plant that many people put in their gardens.

One reason that honeysuckle is popular is that it is resistant to heat and can grow well in all kinds of soil. This makes taking care of the plant very easy. Gardeners typically find that the honeysuckles they plant need little care at all. This allows gardeners to spend more time tending to other plants in their gardens to make them look as nice as possible.

Honeysuckles that are vines grow well when they can attach themselves to walls, fences, and other structures. When these harmless plants are in full bloom, their flowers make every garden look more beautiful. The sweet smell of honeysuckle flowers also attracts pollinators such as bees and hummingbirds. This helps make sure there is an abundance of wildlife in any backyard garden.

Vocabulary

- **vine** *n* a plant with a long stem that grows on the ground or attaches itself to other structures
- **shrub** *n* a woody plant smaller than a tree
- **botanist** *n* a scientist who specializes in the study of plants
- **resistant** *adj* able to stand against or to oppose
- **harmless** *adj* unable to hurt or injure someone or something
- **in full bloom** *phr* full of flowers, as in a tree
- **pollinator** *n* an animal such as an insect that spreads pollen from plant to plant
- **abundance** *n* a large number or amount of something

◪ Outlining

Write an outline of the reading passage in the space provided.

Main Point _____

Argument ❶ _____

_____

_____

Argument ❷ _____

_____

_____

◪ Summarizing Exercises

Read the following sentences. Then, complete the summaries below. The summaries should include the key information in the original sentences.

1 It grows in the wild, but it is also a popular plant that many people put in their gardens.

→ Some people like to _____.

2 This makes taking care of the plant very easy. This allows gardeners to spend more time tending to other plants in their gardens to make them look as nice as possible.

→ Honeysuckle is easy _____, so gardeners can

_____.

3 When these harmless plants are in full bloom, their flowers make every garden look more beautiful. The sweet smell of honeysuckle flowers also attracts pollinators such as bees and hummingbirds.

→ Blooming honeysuckles _____ and

_____.

B Listening Lecture A17

Listen to a lecture on the topic you just read about. Be sure to take notes while you listen.

Note-Taking

Main Point ______________________________

Argument ❶ ______________________________

____

____

Argument ❷ ______________________________

____

____

Summarizing Exercises

Read the following sentences. Then, complete the summaries below. The summaries should include the key information in the original sentences.

1 In recent years, people have started planting honeysuckles in gardens. Well, uh, I strongly advise against that.

→ People should avoid ______________________________.

2 Honeysuckle vines spread far and wide, so they choke other plants and block sunlight. As a result, many plants around honeysuckles in gardens tend to die unless gardeners spend lots of time pruning honeysuckle vines.

→ Honeysuckles ________________, so ______________________________.

3 When they wrap around a fence or a wall, they can get into cracks in brick and mortar—and even wood—and literally rip them apart. Honeysuckles can destroy your walls and fences.

→ Honeysuckle vines can ________________, so they ________________

______________________________.

C | Combining the Main Points

Read the following sentences from the reading passage and listening lecture. Then, combine each pair of sentences by using the given patterns.

1 **Reading** One reason that honeysuckle is popular is that it is resistant to heat and can grow well in all kinds of soil. This makes taking care of the plant very easy. Gardeners typically find that the honeysuckles they plant need little care at all.

Listening One problem is that honeysuckle grows quickly and can take over gardens. Honeysuckle vines spread far and wide, so they choke other plants and block sunlight. As a result, many plants around honeysuckles in gardens tend to die unless gardeners spend lots of time pruning honeysuckle vines.

→ **According to the reading passage,** _____

_____ **. However, the professor says that**

_____ .

2 **Reading** Honeysuckles that are vines grow well when they can attach themselves to walls, fences, and other structures. When these harmless plants are in full bloom, their flowers make every garden look more beautiful.

Listening When they wrap around a fence or a wall, they can get into cracks in brick and mortar—and even wood—and literally rip them apart. Honeysuckles can destroy your walls and fences.

→ **The reading passage states that** _____

_____ **. But the**

professor notes that _____

_____ .

D | Completing the Essay

Complete the following sample essay which summarizes the points made in the lecture. Be sure to explain how they cast doubt on specific points made in the reading passage. Use the phrases to help you write your essay.

In his lecture, the professor talks about some reasons that _____

_____.

In doing so, he challenges _____.

First of all, the professor points out that honeysuckles _____

_____. They do

that by _____ and _____

_____. He notes

that gardeners must _____

_____ to prevent this. The professor therefore challenges the argument

in the reading passage. It claims that _____

_____.

Secondly, the professor mentions that honeysuckle vines can _____

_____. They can _____

_____

_____. This means the vines can destroy

_____. This

goes against the argument in the reading passage. It claims that _____

_____.

In suburban areas around the United States, backyard birdfeeders are common sights. There are several advantages to people providing seeds for birds to eat.

In some places—especially in the suburbs—there is not enough food for birds to eat. So when people feed birds, they are helping support local bird populations. This has resulted in populations of many birds greatly increasing. For example, in the early 1950s, there were fewer than 300 house finches in the eastern United States. Thanks largely to birdfeeders though, their numbers grew considerably. Today, more than two hundred fifty million house finches live in North America.

Birdfeeders do not only benefit birds. The people who fill the feeders get hours and hours of enjoyment. Some of them are avid birdwatchers who enjoy identifying the various species of birds that land on their feeders. Others simply like watching different species of birds interact with one another. It is common for birds such as blue jays, grackles, woodpeckers, and robins to eat at feeders at the same time. They would never get that close to one another in the wild though.

A18

Directions You have 20 minutes to plan and write your response. Your response will be judged on the basis of the quality of your writing and on how well your response presents the points in the lecture and their relationship to the passage. Typically, an effective response will be 150-225 words.

Question Summarize the points made in the lecture, being sure to explain how they cast doubt on specific points made in the reading passage.

COPY   CUT   PASTE   Word Count : 0

A | Reading Passage

Read the following passage carefully. Try to understand what the main argument of the passage is.

Urban heat island is a phenomenon which causes the average temperatures in cities to be higher than in nearby rural areas. The primary reason is that heat is captured and retained by buildings, roads, and other manmade structures. Fortunately, there are ways to counter its effects.

One method is to plant trees and other plants on the tops of buildings. The dark roofs of buildings absorb large amounts of heat, making them quite hot. But in many urban centers, people are planting trees on rooftops. They stop sunlight from reaching the roofs and thus prevent buildings from becoming too hot.

Another method is to construct roads with water-permeable substances. Currently, most rainwater on roads simply runs off the sides. But new technology has created water-permeable concrete and asphalt. Now water can be absorbed by roads, which helps cool them off. The water also seeps into the ground beneath the roads. This provides grass and trees on the sides of roads with water, which helps them grow. As the trees become taller, they provide shade to prevent roads from being hit by direct sunlight. This also helps decrease temperatures in urban areas.

Vocabulary

- **phenomenon** n a fact or event that can be observed
- **retain** v to keep or preserve
- **counter** v to go against
- **absorb** v to soak up or take in
- **water-permeable** adj capable of being penetrated by water
- **asphalt** n a dark, natural substance that is often used to make roads
- **seep** v to pass or flow through something
- **shade** n darkness caused by the blocking of the sun's light

◢ Outlining

Write an outline of the reading passage in the space provided.

Main Point _____

Argument ❶ _____

_____

_____

_____

Argument ❷ _____

_____

_____

_____

◢ Summarizing Exercises

Read the following sentences. Then, complete the summaries below. The summaries should include the key information in the original sentences.

1 Urban heat island is a phenomenon which causes the average temperatures in cities to be higher than in nearby rural areas. Fortunately, there are ways to counter its effects.

→ It is possible to _____

_____ so that _____.

2 But in many urban centers, people are planting trees on rooftops. They stop sunlight from reaching the roofs and thus prevent buildings from becoming too hot.

→ By _____, sunlight

cannot _____.

3 But new technology has created water-permeable concrete and asphalt. Now water can be absorbed by roads, which helps cool them off.

→ Using _____ can help

keep roads cool.

B | Listening Lecture 🎧 A19

Listen to a lecture on the topic you just read about. Be sure to take notes while you listen.

▨ Note-Taking

Main Point _____

Argument ❶ _____

_____

_____

Argument ❷ _____

_____

_____

▨ Summarizing Exercises

Read the following sentences. Then, complete the paraphrases below. The paraphrase should include the key information in each sentence.

1 Nowadays, people are trying to come up with ways to reduce temperatures in cities. Sadly, many of their ideas are flawed.

→ The ideas people have on _____

_____ are flawed.

2 You see, that high off the ground, it's very windy. The soil the trees grow in is also thin. After all, you can't put a meter or two of dirt on rooftops. Because of those two issues, trees on rooftops just don't grow well.

→ Rooftops _____ ,

so trees _____ .

3 But, well, let's not forget that cities have limited budgets. Our city can't rip up all the roads and repave them with water-permeable asphalt. There's not enough money to do that.

→ It is too _____ .

C | Combining the Main Points

Read the following sentences from the reading passage and listening lecture. Then, combine each pair of sentences by using the given patterns.e given patterns.

1 `Reading` One method is to plant trees and other plants on the tops of buildings. The dark roofs of buildings absorb large amounts of heat, making them quite hot. But in many urban centers, people are planting trees on rooftops. They stop sunlight from reaching the roofs and thus prevent buildings from becoming too hot.

`Listening` I'm sure you've seen some buildings in town with trees planted on their roofs. That's actually a great idea . . . but, um, it's not effective. You see, that high off the ground, it's very windy. The soil the trees grow in is also thin. After all, you can't put a meter or two of dirt on rooftops. Because of those two issues, trees on rooftops just don't grow well.

→ **The reading passage argues that** _____

_____ **. But the professor mentions that**

_____ **.**

2 `Reading` Another method is to construct roads with water-permeable substances. Currently, most rainwater on roads simply runs off the sides. But new technology has created water-permeable concrete and asphalt. Now water can be absorbed by roads, which helps cool them off.

`Listening` Our city can't rip up all the roads and repave them with water-permeable asphalt. There's not enough money to do that.

→ **While the reading passage argues that** _____

_____ **, the professor points out that** _____

_____ **.**

D Completing the Essay

Complete the following sample essay which summarizes the points made in the lecture. Be sure to explain how they cast doubt on specific points made in the reading passage. Use the phrases to help you write your essay.

The reading passage describes two ways to _____

_____ . But the professor shows

_____ .

To start, the professor challenges the argument that _____

_____

_____ . She points out that there is too much

_____ . She adds that rooftop trees

do not grow well because _____ .

Because of those two reasons, she states that _____

_____ .

In addition, the professor loves the idea of _____

_____ . The reading passage points out that

rainwater can _____ . It can _____

_____ , too.

They can further _____ . But the professor says that

_____ . Her city cannot _____

_____ .

So the proposed solution will not _____ .

In the Pacific Ocean, there is an enormous pile of floating garbage. More than three times the size of France, the Great Pacific Garbage Patch is the name people have given it. Currently, an effort is underway to remove the garbage.

The name of the effort is the Ocean Cleanup Project. In 2019, a floating device 600 meters long began collecting garbage in the patch for the first time. One advantage of the system is that it can collect not only big pieces of garbage but also tiny microplastics a mere millimeter in size. This kind of efficiency guarantees that the garbage will be almost entirely removed from the ocean.

The managers of this ambitious project hope to eliminate fifty percent of the garbage in the Great Pacific Garbage Patch within the first five years. Then, they expect to collect more than ninety percent of the garbage in it by 2040. By removing the plastic, the project can get rid of a large amount of pollution from the ocean and help restore the ocean habitat for untold numbers of fish and other animals.

A20

Directions You have 20 minutes to plan and write your response. Your response will be judged on the basis of the quality of your writing and on how well your response presents the points in the lecture and their relationship to the passage. Typically, an effective response will be 150-225 words.

Question Summarize the points made in the lecture, being sure to explain why they cast doubt on specific points made in the reading passage.

COPY   CUT   PASTE   Word Count : 0

Part **B**

Independent Writing Task

Independent Writing Task

About the Question

The Independent Writing Task requires you to read a question and then to write an essay about the question. Many questions present a statement and ask you if you agree or disagree with it. You should then choose and write an essay expressing your opinion. Other questions present you with a situation and two choices. You should select one and then write your essay. Recently, some questions present you with a situation and provide you with three choices. You should select one of the three and then write your essay. You will be given 30 minutes to write your essay. Your essay should be more than 300 words. Try to make your essay between 300 and 400 words. That will be long enough to provide enough examples and short enough to give you plenty of time to proofread your essay when you finish it. The ideal essay has an introduction, a body, and a conclusion. The introduction should describe your opinion. The body should contain either two or three paragraphs that present separate points or arguments. It is more common to use three separate points or arguments than two. Be sure to provide examples to support your arguments. And the conclusion should summarize the points that you made in the body.

There are three possible writing tasks you will be presented with, but they all ask you to express your opinion about an important issue.

For the agree/disagree type, the task will be presented in the following way:

- Do you agree or disagree with the following statement?
  [*A sentence or sentences that present an issue*]
  Use specific reasons and examples to support your answer.

  cf. This question type accounts for most of the essay topics that have been asked on the TOEFL® iBT so far.

For the preference type, the task will be presented in the following way:

- Some people prefer X. Others prefer Y. Which do you prefer? Use specific reasons and examples to support your choice.

For the opinion type, the task will be presented in the following way:

- [*A sentence or sentences that state a fact*]
  In your opinion, what is one thing that should be . . . ? Use specific reasons and examples to support your answer.

Directions Read the question below. You have 30 minutes to plan, write, and revise your essay. Typically, an effective response will contain a minimum of 300 words.

Question Do you agree or disagree with the following statement?

Everyone should attend a college or a university after finishing high school.

Use specific reasons and examples to support your answer.

Sample Essay

In my opinion, college and university are important. So I think everyone should attend one after finishing high school. I therefore agree with the statement.

First, people can learn more by attending a college or a university. Students learn plenty during elementary, middle, and high school. But there is so much more information for them to learn. If they attend a college or a university, they can focus on one or two subjects. Then, they can get in-depth knowledge of those subjects. My sister is currently attending a university. She is majoring in chemistry. She took chemistry in high school, but she is learning more about it at her school. She told me that she is so happy she decided to go to her university.

Second, attending a college or a university can help people get better jobs. These days, many jobs require a college or university degree. If a person lacks one, the company will not consider that individual for a job. It does not matter how smart the person is. He or she still needs to have a degree. My cousin is very smart, but he never went to college. He has gotten rejected for jobs many times because of that. He recently decided to attend college next year so that he can try to find a good job in the future.

People can learn a lot at colleges and universities. They can also get better jobs if they have a degree. For those two reasons, I agree with the statement.

Chapter 01

A | Brainstorming

Read the question below and brainstorm your ideas.

Question

Do you agree or disagree with the following statement?

Students should get part-time jobs to help pay for their school.

Use specific reasons and examples to support your answer.

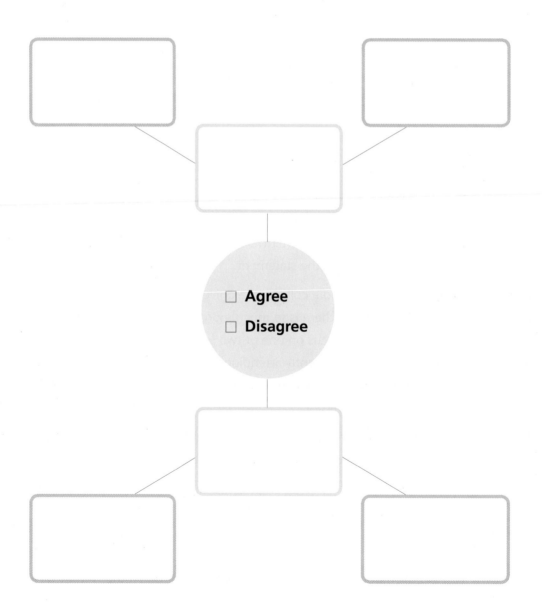

☐ **Agree**

☐ **Disagree**

B | Outlining

Complete the following outline based on your brainstorming map.

Thesis Statement

First Supporting Idea

Topic Sentence:

Supporting Example(s):

Second Supporting Idea

Topic Sentence:

Supporting Example(s):

Conclusion

C | Completing the Essay

Complete the following sample essay. Use the phrases to help you write your essay.

Agree

I agree with the statement. I believe that _____

_____. There are two reasons why I feel this way.

First of all, _____

_____

_____

_____

_____

Second, _____

_____

_____

_____

_____

_____. I therefore agree with the statement.

Disagree

I do not agree with the statement. I do not believe _____

_____ . As a matter of fact, I feel that having a part-

time job can harm students.

For one thing, _____

_____

_____

_____

For another thing, _____

_____

_____

_____

I disagree with the statement for two reasons. _____

_____ . And _____

_____ .

iBT Practice Test

Directions   Read the question below. You have 30 minutes to plan, write, and revise your essay.

Question   Do you agree or disagree with the following statement?

It is hard for teachers to be popular and teach effectively at the same time.

Use specific reasons and examples to support your answer.

COPY   CUT   PASTE   Word Count : 0

A | Brainstorming

Read the question below and brainstorm your ideas.

Question

Do you agree or disagree with the following statement?

People in the past had healthier diets than people do today.

Use specific reasons and examples to support your answer.

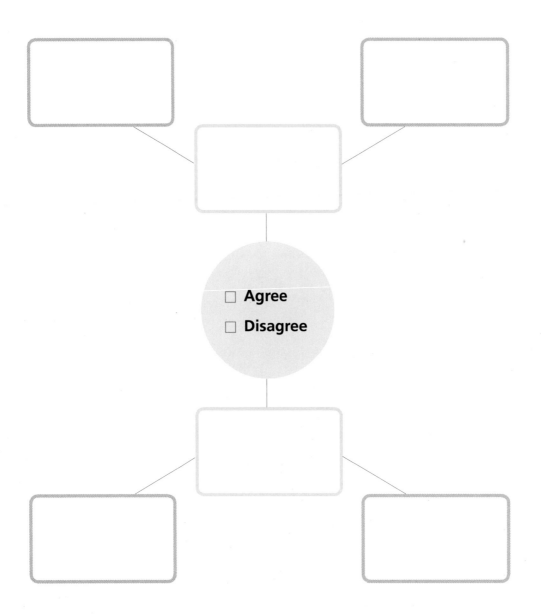

☐ **Agree**

☐ **Disagree**

B | Outlining

Complete the following outline based on your brainstorming map.

Thesis Statement

First Supporting Idea

Topic Sentence:

Supporting Example(s):

Second Supporting Idea

Topic Sentence:

Supporting Example(s):

Conclusion

C | Completing the Essay

Complete the following sample essay. Use the phrases to help you write your essay.

Agree

I definitely _____. People in the past had _____

than people do today. There are two points _____.

For starters, _____

_____

_____

_____

_____

In addition, _____

_____

_____

_____

_____

_____

People in the past _____. They also _____

_____. For those two reasons, I agree with the statement.

Disagree

Many people will probably agree with the statement. However, _____.

In fact, I disagree with the statement for two important reasons.

Nowadays, _____

_____

_____

_____

_____

Another factor to consider is _____

_____

_____

_____

_____

I do not agree with the statement. These days, _____

_____.

So I do not believe that people in the past had healthier diets than people today do.

Directions Read the question below. You have 30 minutes to plan, write, and revise your essay.

Question Do you agree or disagree with the following statement?

People today are busier than people were a hundred years ago.

Use specific reasons and examples to support your answer.

COPY   CUT   PASTE   Word Count : 0

A | Brainstorming

Read the question below and brainstorm your ideas.

Question

Some people believe that universities should provide a good healthcare system for their students. Others believe that students should be responsible for their own health care. Which do you prefer? Use specific reasons and examples to support your answer.

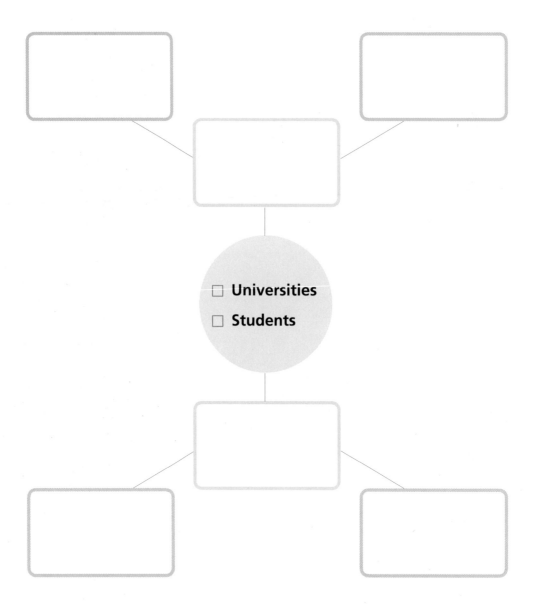

☐ **Universities**

☐ **Students**

B | Outlining

Complete the following outline based on your brainstorming map.

Thesis Statement

First Supporting Idea

Topic Sentence:

Supporting Example(s):

Second Supporting Idea

Topic Sentence:

Supporting Example(s):

Conclusion

C | Completing the Essay

Complete the following sample essay. Use the phrases to help you write your essay.

Universities Provide Health Care

Of the two choices, I prefer the first one. I do not believe that _____

_____. Instead, I believe that _____

_____.

The first reason is that _____

_____

_____

_____

_____

_____

The second reason is that _____

_____

_____

_____

_____

_____

_____. For those two

reasons, I think universities ought to provide a good healthcare system for their students.

Students Provide Health Care

Having universities provide health care for their students sounds interesting. But I think

that _____ .

I feel this way for two reasons.

Firstly, _____

_____

_____

_____

_____

_____

Another advantage is that _____

_____

_____

_____

_____

_____

_____

_____ . For those two

reasons, I think students, not universities, should provide their own health care.

Directions   Read the question below. You have 30 minutes to plan, write, and revise your essay.

Question   Some people like to play sports after school. Others prefer to do volunteer work. Which do you prefer? Use specific reasons and examples to support your answer.

COPY   CUT   PASTE   Word Count : 0

A Brainstorming

Read the question below and brainstorm your ideas.

Question

Do you agree or disagree with the following statement?

Only movies that teach lessons for real life are worth seeing.

Use specific reasons and examples to support your answer.

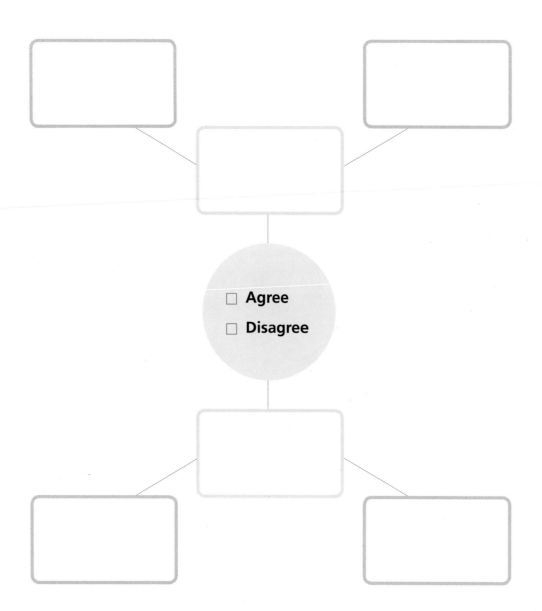

B | Outlining

Complete the following outline based on your brainstorming map.

Thesis Statement

First Supporting Idea

Topic Sentence:

Supporting Example(s):

Second Supporting Idea

Topic Sentence:

Supporting Example(s):

Conclusion

C | Completing the Essay

Complete the following sample essay. Use the phrases to help you write your essay.

Agree

There are many movies being made around the world every year. However, most of them are not worth watching. I therefore agree with the statement because _____

_____ .

_____

_____

_____

_____

_____

Another factor is that _____

_____

_____

_____

_____ .

In addition, _____ .

For those two reasons, I fully agree with the statement.

Disagree

I strongly disagree with the statement. It is not necessary for movies _____

_____. I believe there are other reasons people can watch movies.

The primary reason is that _____

_____

_____

_____

_____

A second reason is that _____

_____

_____

_____

_____

_____

_____. For those two reasons, I disagree with the statement.

Directions   Read the question below. You have 30 minutes to plan, write, and revise your essay.

Question   Do you agree or disagree with the following statement?

It is more fun to watch a sporting event in person than to see it on television.

Use specific reasons and examples to support your answer.

COPY	CUT	PASTE		Word Count : 0

A | Brainstorming

Read the question below and brainstorm your ideas.

Question

Some people believe that traveling is the best way to meet people. Others prefer to meet people by doing community activities. Which method do you prefer? Use specific reasons and examples to support your answer.

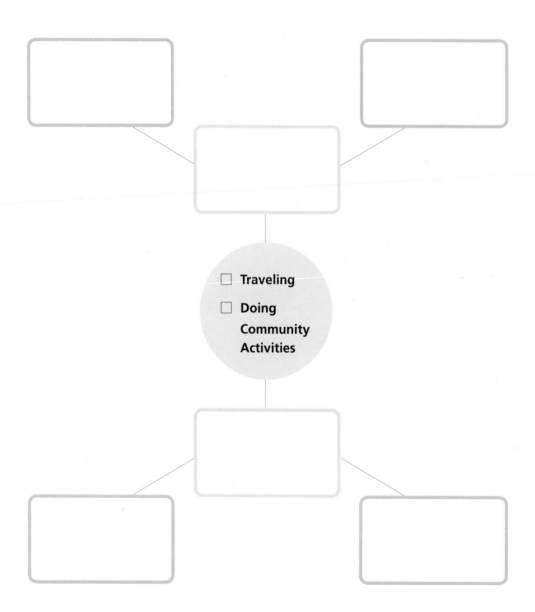

B | Outlining

Complete the following outline based on your brainstorming map.

Thesis Statement

First Supporting Idea

Topic Sentence:

Supporting Example(s):

Second Supporting Idea

Topic Sentence:

Supporting Example(s):

Conclusion

C | Completing the Essay

Complete the following sample essay. Use the phrases to help you write your essay.

Traveling

Of the two choices, I prefer _____. Traveling is a much better way to meet people

than _____.

First of all, _____

_____

_____

_____

_____

_____

Secondly, _____

_____

_____

_____

_____

_____

_____

_____

_____

Doing Community Activities

I have met some people while traveling. But that is not the best way to meet people.

Instead, the best way is _____. I believe this for two

reasons.

The main reason is that _____

_____

_____

_____

_____

Another reason meeting people while doing community activities is great is that _____

_____

_____

_____

_____

_____

_____

_____

> **Directions** Read the question below. You have 30 minutes to plan, write, and revise your essay.

Question Some people like to plan the details of their trips. Others prefer to decide what to do while they are on their trips. Which do you prefer? Use specific reasons and examples to support your answer.

COPY	CUT	PASTE		Word Count : 0

A | Brainstorming

Read the question below and brainstorm your ideas.

Question

Do you agree or disagree with the following statement?

The rules of society today are too strict for young people.

Use specific reasons and examples to support your answer.

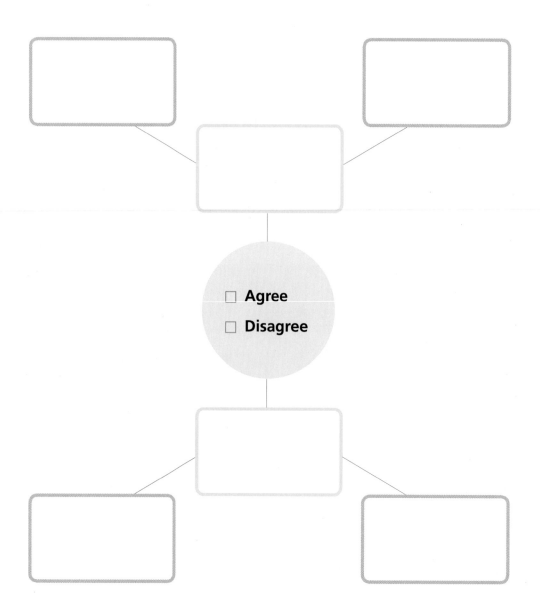

☐ **Agree**

☐ **Disagree**

B | Outlining

Complete the following outline based on your brainstorming map.

Thesis Statement

First Supporting Idea

Topic Sentence:

Supporting Example(s):

Second Supporting Idea

Topic Sentence:

Supporting Example(s):

Conclusion

C | Completing the Essay

Complete the following sample essay. Use the phrases to help you write your essay.

Agree

These days, the rules of society are very strict. They are especially _____

_____. I therefore agree with the statement.

First of all, _____

_____

_____

_____

_____

In addition, _____

_____

_____

_____

_____

_____

_____

_____. As a result, I think that the statement is correct.

Disagree

Many young people claim that _____. However, I

disagree with them. So _____.

For one thing, _____

_____

_____

_____

For another thing, _____

_____

_____

_____

_____

_____

_____

_____. For those

two reasons, I disagree with the statement.

iBT Practice Test

Directions   Read the question below. You have 30 minutes to plan, write, and revise your essay.

Question   Do you agree or disagree with the following statement?

Your job has a greater effect on your happiness than your social life.

Use specific reasons and examples to support your answer.

Word Count : 0

Chapter 07

A | Brainstorming

Read the question below and brainstorm your ideas.

Question

Do you agree or disagree with the following statement?

The more money a person has, the more that person should give away to charity.

Use specific reasons and examples to support your answer.

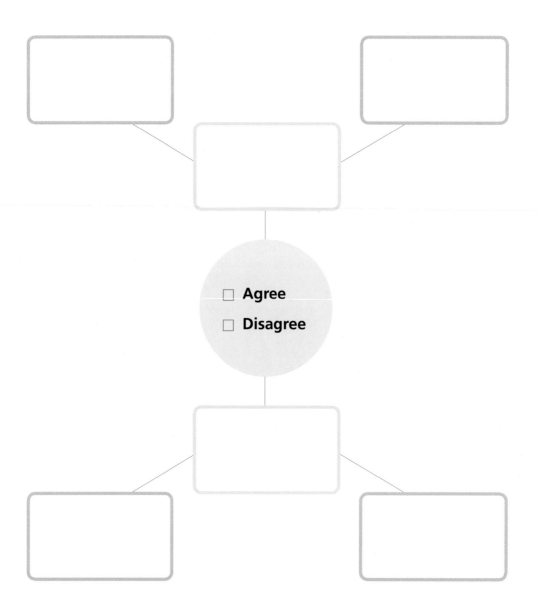

☐ **Agree**

☐ **Disagree**

B | Outlining

Complete the following outline based on your brainstorming map.

Thesis Statement

First Supporting Idea

Topic Sentence:

Supporting Example(s):

Second Supporting Idea

Topic Sentence:

Supporting Example(s):

Conclusion

C | Completing the Essay

Complete the following outline based on your brainstorming map.

Agree

I strongly agree with the statement. The more money a person has, the more _____

_____ .

First of all, people with lots of money can _____

_____

_____

_____

_____

_____

In addition, rich people who give money to charity can _____

_____

_____

_____

_____

_____

Rich people can _____ . They can also _____

_____ . I therefore agree that the more money a person has,

the more that person ought to give away to charity.

Disagree

The statement sounds like a nice idea. However, _____. I do not believe that

_____ .

First, _____

_____

_____

_____

_____

Second, _____

_____

_____

_____

_____

_____ .

Because of those two reasons, I disagree with the statement.

iBT Practice Test

Directions   Read the question below. You have 30 minutes to plan, write, and revise your essay.

Question   Do you agree or disagree with the following statement?

It is more important to focus on happiness than on making money.

Use specific reasons and examples to support your answer.

COPY	CUT	PASTE	Word Count : 0

A | Brainstorming

Read the question below and brainstorm your ideas.

Question

Which of the following abilities do you think is the most important for teachers: the ability to give students advice for the future, the ability to provide students with help in the classroom, or the ability to encourage students to learn by themselves outside the classroom? Use specific reasons and examples to support your answer.

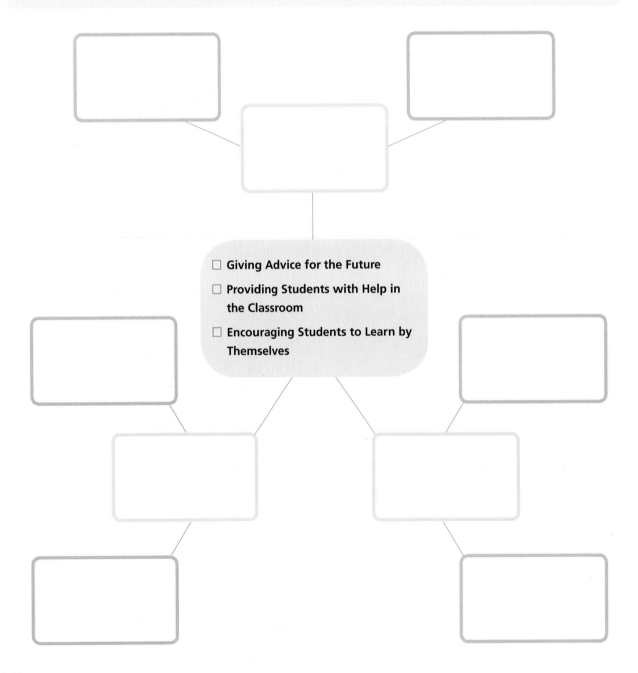

- ☐ Giving Advice for the Future
- ☐ Providing Students with Help in the Classroom
- ☐ Encouraging Students to Learn by Themselves

B | Outlining

Complete the following outline based on your brainstorming map.

Thesis Statement

First Supporting Idea

Topic Sentence:

Supporting Example(s):

Second Supporting Idea

Topic Sentence:

Supporting Example(s):

Third Supporting Idea

Topic Sentence:

Supporting Example(s):

Conclusion

Completing the Essay

Complete the following sample essay. Use the phrases to help you write your essay.

Giving Advice for the Future

All three abilities are important. But the most important ability for high school teachers is

_____ .

One reason is that _____

_____

_____

_____

Another reason is that _____

_____

_____

_____

A third reason is that _____

_____

_____

_____

_____

_____ Those three reasons

make me believe the ability to give students advice for the future is crucial for teachers.

Encouraging Students to Learn by Themselves

Of the three choices, I think the third one is the most important. The ability for teachers to encourage their students to learn outside the classroom is vital.

First of all, _____

_____

_____

_____

Second, _____

_____

_____

_____

Third, _____

_____

_____

_____

The ability to encourage students to learn by themselves outside the classroom is crucial. It can _____ . It can _____ _____ . And it can _____ _____ .

iBT Practice Test

Question What is the best way for students to do assignments? Should they do them alone or in a group? Use specific reasons and examples to support your answer.

COPY CUT PASTE   Word Count : 0

A Brainstorming

Read the question below and brainstorm your ideas.

Question

People often have friends they have known for many years. However, sometimes these friends act in ways that make people upset.

Do you agree or disagree that people should end their relationships with old friends when their friends do things they disapprove of? Use specific reasons and examples to support your answer.

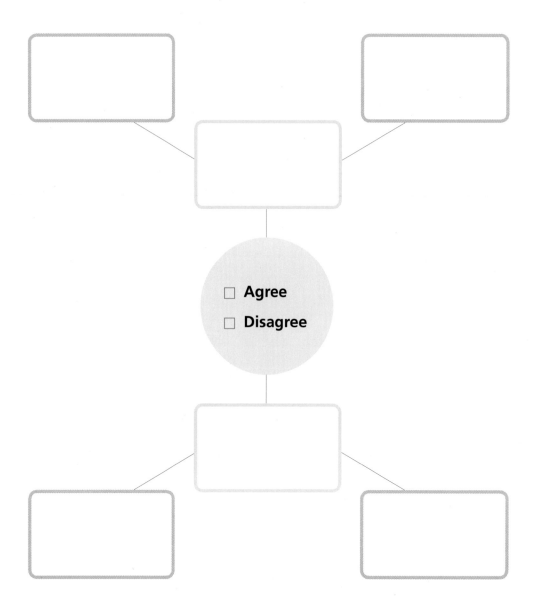

□ **Agree**

□ **Disagree**

B | Outlining

Complete the following outline based on your brainstorming map.

Thesis Statement

First Supporting Idea

Topic Sentence:

Supporting Example(s):

Second Supporting Idea

Topic Sentence:

Supporting Example(s):

Conclusion

C | Completing the Essay

Complete the following outline based on your brainstorming map.

Agree

In my opinion, _____

_____. I agree

with this statement for two reasons.

The first reason is that _____

_____

_____

_____

_____

The second reason is that _____

_____

_____

_____

_____

People should _____

_____

Disagree

I do not support this statement at all. In my opinion, _____

_____

_____

For one thing, _____

_____

_____

_____

_____

For another thing, _____

_____

_____

_____

_____

People can _____

_____

Directions Read the question below. You have 30 minutes to plan, write, and revise your essay. Typically, an effective response will contain a minimum of 300 words.

Question Do you agree or disagree with the following statement?

It is possible for people to be friends even if they have different personalities and interests.

Use specific reasons and examples to support your answer.

COPY	CUT	PASTE		Word Count : 0

A | Brainstorming

Read the question below and brainstorm your ideas.

Question

When people get jobs at companies, they must work a certain number of hours each week. Some people do this by having fixed schedules. So their starting and ending times are the same every day. However, other people like to have flexible schedules, so they have different starting and ending times every day.

Which do you prefer? Use reasons and examples to support your answer.

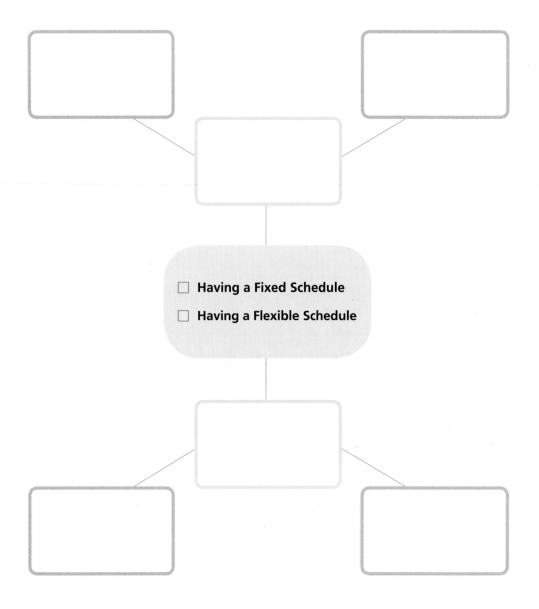

☐ Having a Fixed Schedule

☐ Having a Flexible Schedule

B | Outlining

Complete the following outline based on your brainstorming map.

Thesis Statement

First Supporting Idea

Topic Sentence:

Supporting Example(s):

Second Supporting Idea

Topic Sentence:

Supporting Example(s):

Conclusion

C | Completing the Essay

Complete the following sample essay. Use the phrases to help you write your essay.

Having a Fixed Schedule

Of the two choices, the one I would select is _____

_____

_____

First, _____

_____

_____

_____

_____

Second, _____

_____

_____

_____

_____

_____

_____ .

I would therefore prefer to have a fixed schedule at my job.

Having a Flexible Schedule

Many people love to have fixed schedules at their jobs. But _____

_____

_____

_____

_____

_____

_____

_____

_____

_____

_____

_____

_____

_____

_____. Because of those two reasons,

I would prefer to have a flexible schedule.

Directions   Read the question below. You have 30 minutes to plan, write, and revise your essay. Typically, an effective response will contain a minimum of 300 words.

Question   Starting a job at a company can be difficult for many workers. Some people get assistance by finding mentors to teach them how to do their jobs. However, other people like to learn how to do their jobs by themselves, so they do not ask for any assistance.

Which do you prefer? Use reasons and examples to support your answer.

COPY   CUT   PASTE   Word Count : 0

Actual Test

Writing Section Directions

 Make sure your headset is on.

This section measures your ability to use writing to communicate in an academic environment. There will be two writing tasks.

For the first writing task, you will read a passage and listen to a lecture and then answer a question based on what you have read and heard. For the second writing task, you will answer a question based on your own knowledge and experience.

Now listen to the directions for the first writing task.

Writing Based on Reading and Listening

For this task, you will first have **3 minutes** to read a passage about an academic topic. You may take notes on the passage if you wish. The passage will then be removed and you will listen to a lecture about the same topic. While you listen, you may also take notes.

Then you will have **20 minutes** to write a response to a question that asks you about the relationship between the lecture you heard and the reading passage. Try to answer the question as completely as possible using information from the reading passage and the lecture. The question does **not** ask you to express your personal opinion. You will be able to see the reading passage again when it is time for you to write. You may use your notes to help you answer the question.

Typically, an effective response will be 150 to 225 words long. Your response will be judged on the quality of your writing and on the completeness and accuracy of the content. If you finish your response before time is up, you may click on **NEXT** to go on to the second writing task.

Now you will see the reading passage for 3 minutes. Remember it will be available to you again when you are writing. Immediately after the reading time ends, the lecture will begin, so keep your headset on until the lecture is over.

Recently, several countries have been discussing putting colonies on the moon. Colonies could be staging areas for further space exploration. Tourists could visit them, and mining companies could explore the moon for minerals. However, once built, a lunar colony would be incredibly difficult to maintain.

One big issue is water. Humans need water for drinking, cooking, and bathing. The moon has hardly any atmosphere, so it has no weather, rain, or water. Water is also heavy and bulky, so transporting it to the moon may not be possible. There are ways to recycle human urine. But the amount of water produced gets reduced each time it goes through the process. Therefore, urine is not a sustainable source of water.

Food is another issue. All food would have to be flown to the moon or grown there. Nobody has ever grown plants on the moon though. Besides lacking water, the moon gets large amounts of solar radiation. The soil is poor and lacks nutrients, too. These problems would likely prevent plants from growing on the moon. Without a steady source of food, lunar colonists would be in constant danger of starving.

AT01

Directions You have 20 minutes to plan and write your response. Your response will be judged on the basis of the quality of your writing and on how well your response presents the points in the lecture and their relationship to the passage. Typically, an effective response will be 150-225 words.

Question Summarize the points made in the lecture, being sure to explain how they challenge specific claims made in the reading passage.

COPY   CUT   PASTE   Word Count : 0

Recently, several countries have been discussing putting colonies on the moon. Colonies could be staging areas for further space exploration. Tourists could visit them, and mining companies could explore the moon for minerals. However, once built, a lunar colony would be incredibly difficult to maintain.

One big issue is water. Humans need water for drinking, cooking, and bathing. The moon has hardly any atmosphere, so it has no weather, rain, or water. Water is also heavy and bulky, so transporting it to the moon may not be possible. There are ways to recycle human urine. But the amount of water produced gets reduced each time it goes through the process. Therefore, urine is not a sustainable source of water.

Food is another issue. All food would have to be flown to the moon or grown there. Nobody has ever grown plants on the moon though. Besides lacking water, the moon gets large amounts of solar radiation. The soil is poor and lacks nutrients, too. These problems would likely prevent plants from growing on the moon. Without a steady source of food, lunar colonists would be in constant danger of starving.

Writing Based on Knowledge and Experience

For this task, you will write an essay in response to a question that asks you to state, explain, and support your opinion on an issue. You have **30 minutes** to write your essay.

Typically, an effective essay will contain a minimum of 300 words. Your essay will be judged on the quality of your writing. This includes the development of your ideas, the organization of the content, and the quality and accuracy of the language you used to express ideas.

Click on **CONTINUE** to go on.

COPY   CUT   PASTE   Word Count : 0

Directions Read the question below. You have 30 minutes to plan, write, and revise your essay. Typically, an effective response will contain a minimum of 300 words.

Question

Do you agree or disagree with the following statement?

Reading books is a better way to relax than doing physical exercise.

Use specific reasons and examples to support your answer.

Authors

Michael A. Putlack

- MA in History, Tufts University, Medford, MA, USA
- Expert test developer of TOEFL, TOEIC, and TEPS
- Main author of the Darakwon *How to Master Skills for the TOEFL® iBT* series and *TOEFL® MAP* series

Stephen Poirier

- Candidate for PhD in History, University of Western Ontario, Canada
- Certificate of Professional Technical Writing, Carleton University, Canada
- Co-author of the Darakwon *How to Master Skills for the TOEFL® iBT* series and *TOEFL® MAP* series

Decoding the TOEFL® iBT
WRITING Basic NEW TOEFL® EDITION

Publisher Chung Kyudo
Editors Kim Minju
Authors Michael A. Putlack, Stephen Poirier
Proofreader Michael A. Putlack
Designers Koo Soojung, Park Sunyoung

First published in April 2021
By Darakwon, Inc.
Darakwon Bldg., 211, Munbal-ro, Paju-si, Gyeonggi-do 10881
Republic of Korea
Tel: 82-2-736-2031 (Ext. 250)
Fax: 82-2-732-2037

ISBN 978-89-277-0879-7 14740
        978-89-277-0875-9 14740 (set)

www.darakwon.co.kr

Components Student Book / Answer Book
9 8 7 6 5 4 3   24 25 26 27 28